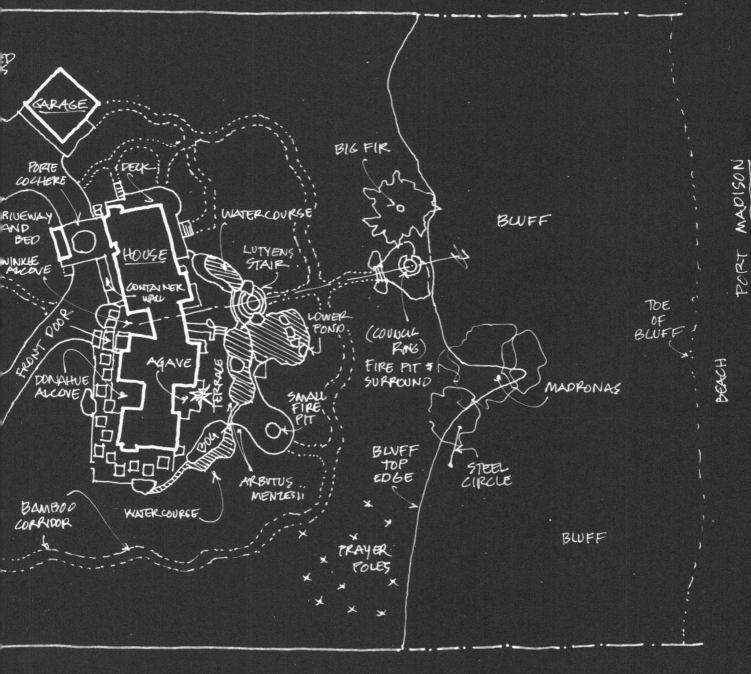

GARAGE

PORTE
COCHERE

BLUEWAY
AND
BED

WINKLE
ALCOVE

DECK

HOUSE

CONTAINER
WALL

AGAVE

FRONT DOOR

DONAHUE
ALCOVE

BOG

TERRACE

BAMBOO
CORRIDOR

WATERCOURSE

WATERCOURSE

LUTYENS
STAIR

LOWER
POND

SMALL
FIRE
PIT

ARBUTUS
MENZESII

BIG FIR

BLUFF

(COUNCIL
RING)
FIRE PIT &
SURROUND

BLUFF
TOP
EDGE

PRAYER
POLES

MADRONAS

STEEL
CIRCLE

BLUFF

TOE
OF
BLUFF

PORT MADISON

BEACH

NORTH

Windcliff

Windcliff

A STORY OF PEOPLE, PLANTS, AND GARDENS

Daniel J. Hinkley

**PHOTOGRAPHY BY
CLAIRE TAKACS**

Timber Press
Portland, Oregon

Frontispiece: The personal satisfaction of creating a new house and garden at Windcliff has come from the melding of both entities into one, without overplaying the hand of either. The garden, which appears feral, unmanaged, and inviting from a distance, belies the use of long-adhered-to principles of good garden making that span the season. The house sacrificed easy, accessible, and breathtaking views across the Puget Sound to two mountain ranges by hunkering close to the earth, becoming an extension of the garden without imposing itself on the landscape.

Photo credits appear on page 270.

Published in 2020 by Timber Press, Inc.

The Haseltine Building
133 S.W. Second Avenue, Suite 450
Portland, Oregon 97204-3527
timberpress.com

Printed in China

Text design by Hillary Caudle
Cover design by Mia Johnson
Endpaper map by Robert Jones

ISBN 978-1-60469-901-2

Catalog records for this book are available from the Library of Congress and the British Library.

To Robert.

We did it together.

We did it all right.

Contents

Memory and Process

My guides, Toby and Takin, survey the Mishmi Hills of Arunachal Pradesh, India, and the Brahmaputra Plain far below.

IT HAPPENED IN A TENT IN NORTHERN INDIA while I was eating dinner by myself during a terrifying thunderstorm. It was cold and I took to eating with my gloves on, realizing well into the meal that I was wearing the same gloves that had repeatedly manhandled assorted scat while finding purchase on the steep trail that day. I removed the gloves and briefly looked at the hands illuminated by my headlamp. These were certainly not my hands. These were the hands of an older man, ashen gray, chafed and deeply impressed with jetties and ebbs. These were hands I had never seen before.

I have been haunted most of my life by an alarmingly good memory, or at least when the memories I adhere to serve my purposes. I inherited this defect from my mother, minutia proud, who could recite conversations, places, menus, and scents seven decades later. Yet this was stolen from her during her eighth decade. Intuitively knowing that my collection of meaningless happenings too would dissolve from view, I realized in this tent on that night that should I remember them, they would soon need to be written.

And now, years since that moment with a headlamp in a frigid tent in India seeing old hands where I had remembered young hands, it is time to muster an attempt. If not a real story from the many inchoate moments of my life elided between the covers of a book, then at least notes to myself as to how my gardens came to be. Recorded now, while my memories of plants—of where I have seen them grow, of how I have coveted them, repeatedly killed them, and occasionally succeeded with them—are still intact for the moment. As are the inspirations that determined ultimately where they might grow. And plants possess their own stories that I can extract and repurpose as my own.

Botanically inspired travel has made me a better gardener—learning where plants grow, what they grow with, what they are pollinated by, and how they are dispersed. The *totius orbis terrarum* generally not considered while in the checkout line at the local garden center has made me a better teacher, a better communicator about plants. These experiences have certainly been motivating when it has come to putting plants together in the garden.

On many levels, I believe my garden at Windcliff is an attempt to evoke a multitude of moments in my life, my personal geography, my own intervals of space and time. It is the recollection of these moments, the relationships and

The Hinkley farm, now 125 years in the same family, is where I opened an Aladdin's cave in the fields, woods, bogs, and beaver ponds of my youth.

When I was five, my mother transplanted a rooted branch of a double-flowered mock orange, *Philadelphus* 'Virginal', from her father's garden. A layered branch from her specimen is thriving at Windcliff today.

memories conjured forth from a simple walkabout, that I have found to be the most gladdening aspect of what I have created.

I was raised in a small town called Evart in north central Michigan. Evart sat tucked amidst weathered hills, bogs, cedar swamps, and tired farmland, with birch and bleached grasses in winter competing with decrepit barns of silvered wood and silos no longer used. My parents did not garden, yet both were intimate with the land and the landscapes that enveloped us.

In the yard surrounding our house, painted by my mother a not-so-subtle shade of red that rattled the community, arose a single yellow tulip and orange oriental poppies. There were lilies of the valley (*Convallaria majalis*) and double-flowered mock orange (*Philadelphus* 'Virginal'). In her own need for an olfactory recall of her childhood, my mom had when I was very young brought a rooted branch of this latter plant from her father's garden, having longed for its perfume in spring.

My mother's father, William Yunk, a mirror maker, lived in a decidedly distilled Germanic community on the shores of northern Lake Michigan in a village called Arcadia. The temperatures there were cooled by the lake in summer and moderated to less frigid in winter. This grandparent, the only one of four who was still alive when I was born, grew primroses, the even then ubiquitous grocery store hybrids that were impossible for us to grow in Evart. He loved his flowers; this I already understood before he died when I was seven years old.

My parents were married in the Lutheran church in Arcadia. The tall white clocked steeple rose above the sugar maples of the village, an effervescent thrusting of summer greens, unabashedly mawkish when the leaves flashed to oranges and reds in autumn.

Before my father, Ralph K. Hinkley, appeared on the scene, my mother was to be married to a childhood sweetheart in the same church with its towering steeple of white. They were both in the Pacific during WWII, reconnoitering on occasion in Okinawa, where she was stationed as a nurse after the Japanese surrender, at a time when wars seemed to have the sense to end. They returned to their village with its pacifying pulse of Lake Michigan, an omnipotent, ceaseless sound that echoed in slaps and smacks on a porch directly across the street from the church, the porch upon which my mother sat the night before her wedding when she learned of the death of her betrothed in an auto accident. The tragedy would propel ceaselessly into our future like unstoppable waves.

The fire-engine-red house in Evart was shaded by box elders (*Acer negundo*) and a single silver maple (*Acer saccharinum*). One of the box elders had a substantial cant to the east. Our dog, Mitzi, once chased a squirrel into its upper branches, and the volunteer fire department was called to get her down. In autumn, the leaves were neatly piled along the street and burned into frosty air on homecoming weekends, the smoke gathered with the bitter smells of chrysanthemums and fermented pears crushed by passing cars.

At night, when my mother would bring us from the depths of dreams with her agonizing screams, like those of a wounded animal, shouting into the blackness a man's name that was not our father's name, my older brother and I would look at each other and wonder. It was then that I began my diversions of learning to identify the birds of our region, its butterflies and reptiles, and mostly its plants—trees of the forests, shrubs and herbs of the ubiquitous peat bogs that peppered our landscapes.

My dad was the village pharmacist and worked six and a half days a week, from 8 a.m. to 9 p.m. every day except Sunday, when he closed the store at 1 p.m. We crammed the things of father and mother, sons and daughter into one afternoon a week as our family unit limped forward emotionally, erecting a hollow reliquary that was hand polished to appear from a distance very normal. On one afternoon each week, I learned from my father—himself a third-generation farmer from the same village—to distinguish hop hornbeams from blue beech, sugar from red maples, swamp white from scarlet oak, sumac from witch hazel. We gathered up buckets of night crawlers for fishing when at last the warm rains of spring arrived and listened to the drumming of ruffed grouse and nighthawks in controlled dives in summer when the air was permeated by the fragrance of sweet fern.

I planted the seeds of grapefruits and oranges, and my father gave me the tops of carrots to place in potpie tins. I waited and watched the seeds germinate and the carrot tops force new growth. Inside, I grew moss and ferns. I cared for monarch butterfly larvae, watching as they spun a bejeweled jade chrysalis with a golden zipper on dying branches of milkweed. Everything in the chrysalis seemed to turn to liquid and then back to solid again with bright orange wings that unfurled like carrot tops. I did not understand then how a butterfly could possibly be reconstituted from liquid. I don't understand it still. I had been hijacked in my youngest self into a world in which I could live alone with an inquisitiveness that did not require explanations.

Directly across the street from our home was a quintessential midcentury florist with a range of greenhouses in which grew carnations and roses for cutting, along with a jungle of tropical plants. The owners, Mr. and Mrs. Shore, assuredly shared whispered imprecations each time I entered their *terra mirantibus* with a litany of questions demanding immediate answers while they were frantic in preparation for a funeral or wedding. This is probably the appropriate place to admit there was more than one reason I chose to study the world around me solo; I was a very odd child.

It was not too shabby a foundation for a young lad obsessed with those things outside his back door. My synaptic faculties for absorbing botanical Latin were unwittingly enhanced by winter months spent perusing the Gurney's and Ferry-Morse seed catalogs—and, of course, the kitschy Sunday inserts of the Michigan Bulb Company, whose metrics for flower-and-fruit-size comparisons always involved children's heads.

Despite the inner boil of something that was never right, my youth was fashioned in a thing miraculously natural. I am uncertain if this alchemy of awakeness to the world was preordained and would thus have found the means to reveal itself under other circumstances. I fear to now gamble on that possibility.

I left for undergraduate school at Michigan State University in possession of a more voluminous inventory of disconnected data points than I certainly realized at the time. My four years there were mostly devoted to reorganizing random bundles of information. Once when I returned home around Thanksgiving, while building a deer blind with my dad, I rather proudly—I don't think arrogantly—rattled off a few scientific names of the trees we were cutting, precisely the same ones he had introduced me to years before: *Carpinus caroliniana*, *Ostrya virginiana*, *Hamamelis virginiana*. He was not particularly impressed; in fact, I interpreted his reaction as irritation at the fusillade of irrelevant facts.

It took no genius, especially for a kid honing his abilities to perceive, to understand the perspicuous glances shot between my parents when discussing career options for someone possessing only a pocketful of botanical Latin. Though my parents were generous with financial support of my education and that of my siblings, failure to launch was never an option in our family. I remain grateful that both of them lived long enough to see that I fed myself, and happily, with a passion they allowed me to—perhaps forced me to—unearth so early in my life.

All this may seem superfluous in a book on making a garden. It is important rubble. These shards of memories within memories formed and shaped a child for whom exhilaration from the natural world became his solace and his reason.

So, for the sake of argument, I have made two gardens, both in concert with my husband, Robert L. Jones, although anyone who gardens or designs houses or writes novels knows that only one is truly possible in a lifetime. It is peculiar indeed to find myself at this juncture in my life, at sixty-six years of age, still making both gardens—still making *a* garden.

The first chapter of this garden is called Heronswood, and it begat and continues to beget Windcliff. Without a doubt, both gardens are primarily about

plants. In fact, I once naively believed that Heronswood was nothing more than plants, a litany of Latin on a not-so-inspiring piece of real estate. Not until we understood the sting of betrayal felt by those who had come to love the place when we sold Heronswood and then again when the new owners shuttered it six years later did we realize there was more nuance to the equation. It was a hard lesson to learn for someone who had thought that knowing a plant and growing it well was all that was necessary. Gardens absorb the passions of their makers and evoke like emotions in those who visit them.

Perhaps staying focused and comfortable with that singular abstraction is what allowed Heronswood to evolve beyond a nursery listing of A to Z. Without being remotely aware of the process as it unfolded, and with an

My husband, Robert Jones, and I—shown here with Henri and Babu— have worked in concert to create two gardens.

admittedly heady inventory of possibilities, from an epic-sized bio-dump we chiseled a discernibly cohesive garden that spoke to many people on many different levels. The Germans have a word that seems to distill its essence, all the while making me feel as if I am bloating the importance of what the garden is. *Gesamtkunstwerk* is the work complete, an art form that amalgamates and stimulates all of our senses simultaneously. Perhaps this is the endpoint of all gardens that are passionately observed, coddled, polished, and re-observed.

If it is, and if that is what I have—we have—achieved, then it should be known that virtually none of it came naturally to me. In regard to original thought, the ability to visualize in three dimensions, or the capacity to communicate any idea on paper or canvas, I would be found to be in the lowest possible percentile, in fact at the level of anaerobic silt. My dogs are better visual artists than I am. But I had Robert, a trained architect with remarkable intuition, to grab inchoate thoughts from thin air and help me shape them into a garden.

Still, it was up to me to add color between the lines. Ultimately, I did things enough, and re-did things enough to undo the things I did, to begin to understand the concepts that made me content, that stimulated my senses. This ongoing process has given me proof that it is possible to learn an art form.

I have always been a logophile, despite the fact that I have had little command over words in general. At one time when I was young and very stupid (actually, I was not that young), I believed that I might arrange my words with some degree of originality and verve. Words conjured forth the same sensations I experienced in my garden, which only carried me further afield, into a chaos of adjectives and nouns and adverbs. *Bellibone* and *bucentaur*. *Facinorous* and *framboesia*, *nepenthe* and *nepotation*. I wished to own them all, and in the process I wet the paper in my excitement like a seventy-five-pound Labrador puppy.

I actually once considered myself sufficiently intelligent to create a new word. It turned out to be much more challenging than I had ever imagined. I wished to make a word that described the scent of freshly mown grass on a warm day in late spring. The emissions of lacerated, volatilized chloroplasts united with the exhaust of a four-cycle engine. My attempts, however, resulted only in the merger of two words, words that had already existed. In the end, I settled upon *chlorotosis* after rejecting *chlorofume* and *chlororaroma* (*chloroma* having already been settled upon as a disease of the bones characterized by green tumors). What I had dabbled in was only word hybridization. In truth, creating a new word is much like trying to make an original garden. It is beyond my depth. But in the end, in writing, as with plants in gardening, a quote from Chief Joseph rings true: "It does not require many words to speak the truth."

Still, I have come to love the ordering of words, the pleasure of placing one adjacent to another with a mindful cadence. An entrance well marked;

repetition, energy, and levity—with a good dose of editing. Concluding with a graceful exit and perhaps a thoughtful afterword.

As with my gardening style, my writing is not to everyone's taste, nor will it ever be. I don't care. As much as I may have when I was younger and more stupid, I do not take myself too seriously on either score. I love the process enough to not bother worrying whether it is good or bad. But I do take seriously the individual components, the words, the plants, and the process. Within each is locked the potential of verse, memory, and magic—deserving of appreciation for what they inherently are or might become.

So this book of carefully chosen words on Windcliff is my attempt to convey my thoughts on good gardening as applied to my own climate and surroundings. There is no magic or revelation; it has been said many times before me and more adroitly and in cleaner prose.

There are more approaches, more tricks to the trade, undoubtedly as many as there are good gardeners. Yet the yearning for beauty, whatever that may be, is the same. It is not intentional nor is it fully accidental. There is no endpoint or possession.

Perhaps making a garden remains simply an unending and clever conversation between our past and ourselves. It is the mettle of that tree raised from seed we have longed to have blossom that finally does, the sky gilded with leaves of aspen in autumn, a sunflower that turns its neck from dawn to dusk. It is the caprice to plant a tunnel of laburnum, which I have never done, or create a meadow, which I am trying to do quite unsuccessfully. It is plucking a ripened apple from the tree you planted with your father, or smelling the *Philadelphus* that once grew in your grandfather's garden.

Finding a New Garden

| moved to a youthful land, relatively speaking. And rocky. And annoyingly dry, especially for someone who cut his teeth on a Pacific Northwest portrayed in *Sleepless in Seattle*, otherwise known as the movie in which it never stops raining.

Lay the Land

IT IS HARD TO IMAGINE the audacity of George Vancouver, who in 1792 sailed into the Salish Sea and began claiming and renaming every mountain and water passage for George III and a syndicate of associates. When the *Discovery* dropped anchor in what is now Blakely Harbor on the eastern shore of Bainbridge Island, it would have been *təˈqʷuʔbe*, "mother of waters." Tahoma, looming 14,411 feet above the landscape, commanding the very essence of our

The bluff we first walked upon on the day we purchased the property in June 2000 was overpowering in its possibilities and intimidating in its scale.

region, he called Mount Rainier—a name that, sadly, became official a century later. On certain days, under the right conditions and from particular vantages, the peak appears preposterously huge.

But already here was a rich, colorful, and calibrated culture. They were not people in need of nomenclature for the places where their ancestors fished, hunted, gathered berries, and wove exquisite baskets from the bark of cedar.

The Suquamish on the eastern shores of our peninsula, the S'Klallam to the northwest, and the Skokomish to the south shared their daughters in marriage with one another while creating a healthy harmony in the tradition. Those three communities, though vastly changed, are still intact and vibrant today. Located in Indianola, Windcliff sits within the boundaries of the Port Madison Indian Reservation, authorized for the Suquamish in the Treaty of Point Elliot in 1855. It was a military leader of the Suquamish whose name, Kitsap, was eventually adhered to our county. From the same community, Chief *Si'ahl* is commemorated in the name of the largest city in our state, Seattle, whose skyline we see in the distance from our garden.

Windcliff lies on the northeast side of the Kitsap Peninsula, an impressive, narrow, and derelict pile of rocky debris left behind by retreating glaciers seventeen thousand years ago, only microseconds in a cosmic sense.

Geologists will tell you that residents of this northern end of our county were gifted through this dumping of glacial rubbish with a nonmarketable commodity known as the Vashon Stade, a natural soil formation that is one part loam, three parts sand, and ten parts boulders the size of children's heads. The pH runs neutral to slightly acidic. There is, as you might guess, virtually no water-holding capacity. In fact, as composting of human bodies in lieu of conventional burial has become the new rage in Washington State, my last endeavor as a plantsman may be making the rocky, well-draining topsoil of my garden richer and more nutrient laden.

On the eastern side of this peninsula, the ice-chiseled Puget Sound (also known as the Salish Sea, as it was and is called by our native tribes) plunges to nearly a thousand feet deep. Its waters, with an invigorating average year-round temperature of 49 degrees F, temper the rise and plunge of mercury in our thermometer throughout the calendar. At any time of year, the water feels only slightly warmer than liquid nitrogen, as I know from the few times I have bathed in liquid nitrogen. I blame this frigid bathtub of ice water adjacent to our bluff for my inability to ripen tomatoes. This is a reasonable excuse.

The long stretch of snow-covered peaks farther to the east is the Cascade Range, comprising thousands of extinct and weathered volcanoes extending from British Columbia to northern California. These mountains, too, are relative youngsters, beginning their rise to glory only forty million years ago.

A window seat on any commercial aircraft arriving at or departing from SeaTac allows a full frontal of the peloton of active players in this range, the fire mountains, the gods of the Cascades. Each has an average lifetime of only a million years. Mount Baker, Glacier Peak, Mount Adams, Mount Saint Helens, and Mount Rainier lift their glaciers nearly two miles up into the sky, at least until they blow their peaks a bit higher in a plume of pyroclasts.

The lift of saturated Pacific storms into and above the peaks of the Cascades produces astronomically impressive levels of precipitation found nowhere else on earth. Mount Baker and Mount Tahoma (aka Rainier) regularly trade positions as the world record holder for annual snowfall; Mount Baker currently wears the "white shirt," accepting ninety-five feet of snow during the 1998–99 winter. Yes, feet.

Now take a gander to the right from our south-facing bluff. The opulent Olympic Mountains are the centerpiece of our western skyline. They are segregated from the Kitsap Peninsula by Hood Canal, an ice-carved, narrow, and

Windcliff exists on a rare south-facing promontory jutting into the north-south-running fjord of Puget Sound, two hundred feet above the body of chilled salt water. From its vantage, Tahoma rises directly centered above the entrance to Elliot Bay, Seattle's natural harbor.

extremely deep fjord shared by nuclear submarines, harbor seals, and the orcas that eat them (the seals, that is). Nonvolcanic, they are younger than the Cascades by thirty million years and embraced entirely by Olympic National Park, the largest of its kind in the lower forty-eight. And it is this landform, the Olympics, that is the senior conductor of the climatic symphony that informs the way I garden.

This is not to say that the Cascades don't have some say in the matter. Two breaks in that great Hadrian's Wall of basalt allow seepage of supercooled arctic air into our beloved mild western maritime lowlands. I have a particularly low regard for the northernmost, the Frasier Valley in southern British Columbia, which is generally at fault when things go poorly for us in a bad winter. Canadians, eh? To the south, the Columbia River Gorge, east of Portland, is the curse of serious gardeners of interior Oregon.

But it is the Olympic Range that has the greater effect. Its series of peaks, rising to less than eight thousand feet, are our rain catchers and cloud movers. Storms from the Pacific, dehumidified as air rises and cools, are split in two; varying portions take the southern route, while the remaining head north. Where they meet again, too infrequently right over our property, updrafts and convection lead to a narrow band of significantly increased precipitation, known in Puget Sound-ese as the convergence zone.

Because of this folly, we drag our hoses on a slice of land that exists on the eastern edge of the so-called Olympic rain shadow. Travel due west from where we live for two and a half hours to Forks, Washington, slightly inland from the ocean and home to popular fictionalized bloodthirsty vampires, and you will find a yearly rainfall averaging twelve feet. Yes, feet. About forty miles

The Olympic Range, viewed here from Windcliff, consists of rain-catcher peaks that significantly modify the climate of the greater Puget Sound basin.

northwest of Windcliff, the small town of Sequim averages a paltry sixteen inches of rain annually. By the time the storms converge closer to home, our yearly totals are boosted to a slightly more generous thirty inches per year.

By closer to home, I refer to Indianola, a charming village hugging the shores of the sound accessed by a dead-end road. The village center consists of a general store, post office, and covered pavilion. Indianola is filled with people who love their dogs, with perhaps one or two people who loathe the fact that so many people love their dogs.

It was upon this already rich fabric that the garden of Windcliff was begun. But not by us.

Early Years

MY GARDENING LIFE BEGAN IN MICHIGAN. It has been said that you can't go home again, yet the rule, it seems, does not apply to those with a profound curiosity about the natural world. Fortified with additional data points, those enamored of the fullness of life will rediscover the landscapes of their youth with new eyes on each return to their beginnings. Though seminal moments of my life as a gardener occurred in the woodlots of northern Michigan with sweeps of trillium and lady's slippers, and in autumn fields of asters and goldenrods, going home has only buttressed my knowledge of and appreciation for my youthful surroundings.

I taught high school horticulture in Fremont, Michigan, in the late seventies. After spending summers visiting siblings in Washington, all of whom were part of the great Lutheran western migration, I made the decision to relocate, along with my endearing dog, Emerson, to the Evergreen State. I chose, however, the infrequently green Wenatchee Valley in the high desert east of the Cascades to begin my association with our region. Wenatchee was then, and remains, a dream for those who live to ski, raft, hike, and bicycle or hunt morels.

During this time, I explored the western slope of the Cascades on weekends, equating the two-hour drive over the Cascades in a botanical sense with the drive from Michigan to Florida. Seattle, the ever-opulent Emerald City, ultimately stole my heart and I was accepted into a nascent master's program at the University of Washington in the autumn of 1983. Emerson and I moved that September into the iconic Stone Cottage in Washington Park Arboretum.

In early October of the same year, I had my first date with a man I had met in a gay square dance group called the Puddletown Squares. On a quintessential foggy autumn day, Robert Jones and I manned his two-station rowboat from

Lady's slipper orchid, *Cypripedium reginae,* grows in the moist woodland behind the Hinkley farm in Evart, Michigan.

West Seattle—where Robert lived—across Elliot Bay and along the harbor front of downtown Seattle, negotiating our small boat between ferries departing and arriving from Bainbridge and Bremerton as Emerson performed seal-watching duty from the helm. And somehow, in one of the greatest marvels of life, from that day of dipping oars into dead calm water and foghorns and a warming fire in his cottage after our first full day together, thirty-eight years have evanesced, like an unanticipated gust of wind suddenly carrying away thousands of gilded leaves at their finest moment.

I accepted a position at Bloedel Reserve on Bainbridge Island the day I graduated in June 1985, and Robert and I moved into a small farmhouse that no longer exists on the estate. At that time, the Reserve and its two-hundred-plus acres were not open to the public but maintained for Prentice and Virginia Bloedel, who visited each year for the month of August. We supplied their kitchen with vegetables and eggs from our garden. During the rest of the calendar, the Reserve was our own, our refugia from an immense sadness at the height of the AIDS epidemic. Too many visited us in that storied landscape for the first and only time.

While my tenure at the Reserve was brief, it was bizarrely seminal, with prophetic moments that in retrospect seem to defy simple coincidence, although many would consider them distilled serendipity. One of my highly vaunted responsibilities as maintenance supervisor was to haul loads of trash weekly to the transfer station, also known as the dump, near Hansville, nearly twenty-five miles away. Each week, especially on crystalline days in winter, I would pause at the intersection of Hansville Road and NE 288th Street. From the top of the hill, 288th was a commandingly handsome tree-lined allée revealing in the distance the peaks of the Olympics. As I passed this road each week, I would say to myself quietly or perhaps simply mouth the chimera as in only a game, "That's a road I would live on." Two years later, on September 1, 1987, with Emerson in the back seat, Robert and I opened the gate to our new property and first home. We called it Heronswood on that evening; the home and garden remain at 7530 NE 288th Street today.

Also, just as weirdly, on daydreaming days at the Reserve I would look over the bluff from the front lawn of the main residence and imagine the properties I could see in the distance, cogitating on the vantages of Puget Sound and surrounding landscapes, and formulate pipedreams of gardening there. As I was a newbie to West Sound country, my geography was not well honed. I believed I was looking at the high bluffs of Whidbey Island, in truth many miles to the north. Today, if one were to draw a perpendicular line from the center of the residence as it sits on the Bloedel property, it would nearly precisely dissect the land that was even then called Windcliff.

Heronswood

THE BRAWN AND BRAINS OF WINDCLIFF, Heronswood is a story that requires its own telling. When Robert and I moved there, we brought our meager home furnishings in a single load in a rented U-Haul. The plants and propagules I had amassed over nearly a decade took another six trips in the same truck. As much as Robert may not have understood the dimensions of what I hoped to create, there could be no mistaking my intention. I had always wanted a nursery. We arrived at Heronswood with all the makings while primed to begin looking at plants in the wild.

At the time, I was teaching horticulture to adults—smart adults—at Edmonds Community College. No better student can be found than a teacher. Heronswood is where I sharpened my pencil as a gardener and a plantsman, in part by inquisitiveness but mostly out of necessity.

In the woodland, borders, and potager of that first garden, I learned the principles of placing plant next to plant. For the first five years, as my canine soulmate, Emerson, watched with some degree of concern, there was a frenetic intensity to our lives. Heronswood took flight by my being possessed by something indescribable—something between resolve, rapacity, insistent hunger, and adamant refusal to fail.

The development of the garden at Heronswood went hand in hand with the evolution of the nursery and of my grasp of the plant kingdom. But also, I was a student of gardening in 1990 Seattle, which was heavily weighted toward competitive plantsmanship and a clamant need for precisely pigmented combinations. I don't mean to be disparaging. I bought into it hook, line, and sinker— the color-driven double mixed border and assorted contrivances, following the English straight down the garden path. Many parts of the garden at Heronswood, those most popular with visitors, were sternly controlled and managed. It was in the woodland, however, where I found my true soul in the process of garden making by evoking bits of nature. There is where I learned to own a garden, and I took with me to Windcliff the most valuable lessons acquired.

I evolved a gardener's intuition but never the confidence of a designer. I could only decipher what had happened well, or poorly, after the fact—Monday morning quarterbacking. I never envisioned a road map—at Heronswood or at Windcliff—but instead gardened via exasperatingly long and contradictory conversations.

Heronswood became a laboratory, a hotel and salon, an entrepôt of ideas and new plants with an eclectic guest list of often-celebrated authors, artists, designers, gardeners, and media personalities. It was bigger than its parts, and more than Robert and I and our talented and adored Heronistas could sustain.

The yearly Heronswood catalogs featured covers by commissioned artists, the only requirement being that a heron and a frog appear somewhere in the artwork. The millennial catalog, with artwork by botanical illustrator Jean Emmons, contained thirty-five original essays by noted horticulturists of the time.

By 2000, girdled by staff and smothered in responsibilities, both Robert and I were feeling suffocated by success. Without our having even remotely considered a deliberate plan to extract ourselves from the business, an emancipator from the East Coast appeared like an apparition, with big promises and an even fatter paper bag filled with cash.

The psychopathology of the relationship we ultimately agreed to and endured for the next six years is inexhaustibly rich, but it serves no purpose to rehash or ridicule. It was as if we had picked up a deranged hitchhiker along the road simply because we were famished and he was holding a family-size bucket of Kentucky Fried Chicken, all the while knowing we would be held hostage at knifepoint long after the finger lickin' was finished. We were as culpable in making poor decisions as the purchaser. As a Stephen Sondheim lyric from *Sunday in the Park with George* goes, "I chose and my world was shaken. So what? The choice may have been mistaken. The choosing was not."

On a beautiful spring day in May 2006, I rode my bike from Windcliff to work at Heronswood. An hour later, I rode back through the gates of Windcliff and did not return to Heronswood for six years.

Leaving Heronswood

YEARS AGO, a month after we received a six-week-old English springer spaniel, Robert and I unexpectedly adopted an orphaned four-month-old American cocker. As dogs are known to do, ours have proffered us years of undiluted pleasure along with immense veterinary bills. There is an entire wing of our local pet clinic named in their honor. Yet our only regret in bringing any of our dogs into the family is later having to navigate the loss of their companionship, the natural yet dreaded transition to that point beyond our touch, as each in turn jumps the fence and at last bounds freely away.

Leaving my first garden will ultimately seem to have been a much easier segue, despite my experience at the time of all those clichéd phases of death and dying. I must avoid sounding overly sentimental. We did make the decision to sell Heronswood without any gun held to our heads. But I expected the garden to continue and evolve, that I would have the opportunity to return in my dotage for an incontinent stagger, revisiting saplings that had become trees or a colony of ranunculus that had, at last, reached the proportions of my dreams. I was anticipating my role as the curmudgeon, saying a lot by saying nothing at all while scrutinizing the unavoidable changes that must happen to any garden.

For a while, I was afforded the luxury of two gardens at once—one with a respectable and wise patina of age, perhaps with just a bit of arthritic gimp, and one with the personality of a frisky, badly behaving springer spaniel. I would be able, at least I thought, to let go slowly of the first as I gained devotion to the second. In truth, I did not have a clue how to leave a garden at all. So then, after the sting had subsided, it seemed quite right that the gate was at that time so abruptly shut. I began to see that gardens have a way of following you home like an orphaned puppy dog.

Though an enchanting potting shed, a particularly ancient sugar maple, or a sublime water feature may be left behind in gardens we create, we never abandon the approaches and appreciations we garner along the way. Those are the tutorials that come with us, neatly packed and ready to use. And fortunately for Robert and me, all of our really big mistakes had been left behind.

Astonishingly enough, I would once again face these very mistakes on the same property six years later. In 2012 I accepted the position of director of Heronswood, now owned and operated by the Port Gamble S'Klallam Tribe, who had purchased the property at auction. It was a rare gift, an opportunity to do it right this time and ultimately leave Heronswood with grace.

Windcliff

IN AUTUMN 1999, we had been fully permitted by Kitsap County to build on a high bank waterfront parcel on Hood Canal boasting a magnificent view of the Olympic Range. The property was on a busy road and possessed lifeless, tired soil. It would not be an unproblematic place to garden, nor a quiet place to live.

Two decades earlier on a cloudless June day, Robert and I had visited Peg West and Mary Stech, acquaintances we'd come to know through fundraisers we'd hosted at Heronswood. We had arrived at their property, Windcliff, to help them prune an old specimen of *Acer palmatum* 'Dissectum', the ubiquitous weeping red-leaf Japanese maple. Our visit had lacked even a hint of covetousness. Like standing before Half Dome or the Taj Mahal or the Venus de Milo, one might be filled with awe but never consider possessing such beauty.

For reasons I can't fully recall, before we launched our building project on Hood Canal we wrote Peg and Mary, longtime residents of Indianola, to ask if they knew of any other available nearby properties. They called us the following day, saying we had "thrown them a lifeline." We drove up a steep and snaking narrow lane posted at 12.5 mph and signed papers to purchase their property twenty-four hours later. On that vivid June day, we stood on a turf-covered bluff with a view—the one of impossible dreams—and felt the mirth that comes from the promise of something new and good.

Mature rhododendrons, mostly hybrids of local origin, surrounded the approach to the well-loved home and garden of Peg West and Mary Stech, which they called Windcliff.

Twenty years on after purchasing a parched, mostly lifeless high bluff, the garden at Windcliff continues to approach the ever-moving-end-point of what the owners wished it might be: a garden in which to lose oneself, a place of rediscovery, a personal journey for the guests and gardeners alike to celebrate the joy that comes from the containment of the natural world.

The commencement of a new garden is an exercise in controlled elation—a galvanization of all the things you know you have done right thus far, tempered by the realization that there are a lot of things you are not yet aware of that you are probably going to do wrong. Much, I suppose, like having a second family, when youthful expectancies and anxieties are set aside and contentment is found simply in the process. Contentment, that is, until the arrival of the unanticipated.

Garden Inspiration

SEVERAL YEARS AGO, I watched a movie called *Enchanted April* about a party of English ladies who rent a villa on the northern Italian coast for a month. Even though the house sits directly above the Mediterranean, the views of the water beyond are concealed by a mature, jumbled, and overgrown garden with half-broken pots of pelargoniums on the terrace and paths tumbled by fragrance (the smells are honestly projected onto the screen). Far from being an obtrusive landscape, it is portrayed as a place where spirits are rejuvenated while rediscovering love and hope. Mentally extracted frames from this film became my muse as I navigated the prospects laid out before us.

With the luxury of not having to immediately move onto the property, Robert and I acquainted ourselves with the site for nearly three years before fully committing to any tactic. Watching the sun arc through the sky through each season was pivotal in orienting the house and ultimately creating the garden. Though the previous owners were rambunctious gardeners and had established a refined palette of mature trees and shrubs directly surrounding the existing home, the lion's share of the six-and-a-half-acre property was a sterile slate of turf mown directly to the bluff edge and the fenced boundary lines.

For nearly two decades I had gardened inch by inch. There were no vistas at Heronswood. We were completely concealed by forest, and what we reveled in was found mostly at our feet. Quite suddenly I was gardening mile by mile. Whereas I do not believe all gardens need to confine themselves within the context of place, we simply had no choice but to tackle head-on this expanse of sky, water, and looming volcano. I was acutely aware that I did not wish to create a garden with the primary charge of embellishing a beautiful view. I would need to have it disappeared to make what I was to create stand on its own.

I've learned that every garden space has an inimitable driver, if but a grove of birch in northern Michigan or an outcropping of rock in Arizona; there is an element unique to any property that leads you. In our case, it was our iconic Pacific madrona (*Arbutus menziesii*) that already graced our bluff edge. The hues of the bark of our madronas, resplendent in the light of early morning and late afternoon, inspired the exterior and interior design of our house.

Besides the unknown variables inherent in any potential garden site, there are a few elements of style that we all bring to the table. What type of garden do I want? The answer is generally found not so much in what the site demands as in how we approach our lives. Designing our garden on a grid was anathema to us. Though we live highly structured lives, we also live informally. I wanted an inviting, intimate garden, much like the overstuffed chair next to our fireplace, much like that place of self-discovery along the Mediterranean coast I had seen on the silver screen years before.

The mesmerizing hues of the bark of our native Pacific madrona, *Arbutus menziesii*, provided inspiration for both interior and exterior finishes to the house.

Thresholds and Gates

Still round the corner there may wait,
A new road or a secret gate.

—J.R.R. TOLKIEN

The gates of the family farm of my youth were entirely functional. They opened and closed—often not so easily—in order to keep something or someone in or out. They were vexatious physical barriers separating one field from another.

The evening we took possession of Heronswood in 1987, we threw open the gate and it fell completely off its hinges. A heron in the adjacent pond startled into flight at the sound. At that moment we were gifted with nomenclature for the property. Buddhists would call this liminality, the space between what was and what's next. We thought of it as yet another check to write for repairs.

We rebuilt that gate from the most basic of materials and for the most fundamental of reasons, security. Our nursery was a quarter mile from our home. Yet we came to associate the physical process of opening and closing that aperture with sequestering ourselves from a world that threatened to consume us. It became a ritual of entering and leaving the refuge of home.

When we began the garden at Windcliff, there were again the practicalities of fences and gates to consider, mostly for the exclusion of deer. Robert and I designed a welcoming gate of iron evoking the physics of the property, waves and wind. Though this time we had the means to install a state-of-the-art code-controlled mechanism to do the work for us, we chose instead a very annoying manual latch that requires volumes

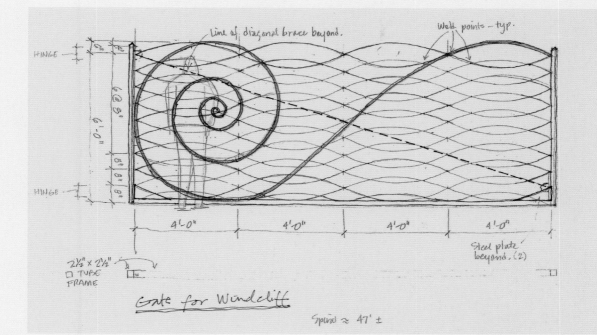

Line of diagonal brace beyond.

Weld points - typ.

HINGE

HINGE

6'-0"

4'-0" 4'-0" 4'-0" 4'-0"

2½" × 2½"
□ TUBE
FRAME

Steel plate
beyond. (2)

Gate for Windcliff

Spiral ≈ 47' ±

of elaborate instructions to operate as well as the exit from a warm, dry vehicle. We wished to retain the ritual of crossing the threshold on foot, leaving the car for but a moment to smell the witch hazels in winter or pull a few weeds in summer, taking time to reflect upon the dispiritedness of leaving or the blessedness of returning, mindful of unknowns in either direction.

TOP · Robert and I together designed a gate that would repeat the leitmotif of wind and waves that was prominently portrayed in the house interior.

The gate was executed in steel by local craftsman Dave Kaster. It demands the ritual of physically entering and departing from the refuge of home.

Design Principles

I have to come clean and break it to you as gently and kindly as I can. My garden is not the one captured in these extraordinary photographs at just the right moment, in the precise light, by a talented artist. It is an improv performance with more days dead in a ditch than anyone could imagine. As gardeners we choreograph our space by the minute, through the days and years, and will never see the same scene twice. I believe we all strive for a bit of drama, mystery, or even comedy in the gardens we create. Yet we're offended when they are described as contrivances. How could they not be? Each year is a slow-cooked reenactment of the year before with sometimes-new actors taking on roles along with returning players giving altered performances. In this there should be no disappointment but only elation that you have a new season ahead to make it better.

Garden as Play

NOTE TO SELF: IT IS STILL A LOT OF WORK.

It really is rather odd, this thought of deliberately putting one plant adjacent to another. The inception of that consideration and its success—in my garden, that is—has more often than not been the result of serendipity, a frivolous comment overheard, or an innocent mistake. The number of times I have taken inspiration from, nurtured and fermented, amended and then executed a composition unearthed from the pages of my library of books dedicated to artful combinations is close to nil. I do freely admit to cutting my teeth on Graham Stuart Thomas's books; early on that is where I dwelled to learn plants, taking to heart his suggestions as to what he might plant, where, and with what.

Whether Mr. Thomas ever actually constructed these combinations in his garden or simply imagined they might be a jolly good idea, I will never be sure. I visited him in his garden shortly before he died, and I did not recognize any of

Oh, take the time to waste a moment.

—KINGS OF LEON, "WASTE A MOMENT"

Two clumps of *Phormium tenax*, collected on Chatham Island in 2010, flank *Nolina longifolia*, adding exclamation while providing a view corridor to the terrace surrounding the kitchen wing of the house.

the pairings he spoke of so gently and genuinely and that I had eagerly appropriated for my first plantings at Heronswood. Paint first by numbers if you must, I say, but then learn to paint broadly outside the lines.

I began gardening critically at Heronswood just as the colorists had retaken dominion of horticultural movements on both sides of the Atlantic. What might have started as gentle play became serious business with legions attempting to outchromatify one another. A whole lot of color shaming went on. I have nothing against studying the color wheel and understanding retreating and advancing hues and tints. Some of my best friends are colorists. However, devotion to this single ideology began to take a bit of shine off the trowel.

Christopher Lloyd seemingly gave a damn about color, though he wrote playfully, sometimes derisively, on his favorite combinations. He understood fully the far more important concerns; color was only a way he could wink at the world to show us how foolish we were in our earnestness.

My apologies to the many other talented designers of the world who took the time to put to paper their precepts of what a garden must be and whose bound volumes I have felt compelled to buy for our library. I have studied them no more than any recipe in the many cookbooks I have also felt compelled to buy. A quick glance at the ingredients, the occasion, the presentation, and the seasonings is as far as I have ever wanted to go. I still add garlic to everything. Peel and seed tomatoes? Not going to happen.

I can recall a seminal moment in my genuine appreciation of the personal journey coursed by everyone who loves to garden. I was somewhere in the deep Midwest with one of the most challenging climates imaginable, giving a presentation about the marvelous plants I grew, all the while knowing the audience

Yucca rostrata and *Y. gloriosa* 'Variegata' flank steps leading from the terrace to the bluff. At lower left, *Rhodanthemum atlanticum*, from North Africa, begins blossoming as early as late January in mild winters.

never would. Along with my many horticultural counterparts across the globe who speak publicly as part of this profession, I am not alone in saying that the most exhausting part of the process is the much-envisaged tour of any region's horticultural high spots before or after the lecture. Being held prisoner by the most hospitable and sincere gardeners conceivable can be excruciatingly painful.

On this particular day, I was treated to lunch at a simple home in the suburbs. Immediately following a quick tour of their collection of Thomas Kinkade paintings came the expected long stroll through their garden. It was precisely what I had imagined it would be, Groundhog's Day all over again, this one perhaps even a tad less tantalizing. As if randomly dropped by a tornado, a stone-lined path led alongside a miniature train system rambling through a collection of dwarf conifers. Each plant was correctly identified on handwritten stakes in the proportion of cemetery monuments.

The moment of acuity came when the pathway ended. It just ended. We turned around into a biting cold wind and resumed discussing the same plants we had just seen, but this time from their backsides. I paused a moment, somewhat incredulously, to study the face of my host. I then recognized his immense pride in his achievements and his sincere devotion to his plant collection. I felt more than ashamed of my judgmental impudence. To find that degree of personal gratification in our own gardens, free from dogmata and tenets, is all we should hope for. Ever since, I have visited as many gardens as I can wherever I am. It is only those that exist devoid of a true gardener that I find perturbing.

Gardening is a lot like skiing. The first two or three times down the hill are going to be forever the most pleasurable, primarily because you are so grateful to still be alive at the bottom of the hill. Once you start to perfect your style the work begins, and it becomes, well, work. Take those first runs slowly, I say, and enjoy every minute. Take the time to waste a moment observing what you have made and dreaming of what you will strive to create. Unlike a picture or a musical recording, what you pause to appreciate will never again be at your avail.

Evaluating Plants and Editing

I RECALL WITH FONDNESS listening to the lectures of Ireland's Helen Dillon. She liked relating that she would take a trip out into her garden each spring and look every plant in the eye and say, "What are you doing for me?" "And if it didn't respond with an answer I believed it should have, then, well, off with its head."

A swath of heath from the original landscape creates a visually quiet zone and is a particularly appealing place for the dogs to scratch their backs.

Unlike the immeasurably talented gardener Ms. Dillon, I have shown a tremendous capacity for putting up with underperformers for much too long. I can justify this in some instances. Throughout my garden there may be an intrinsic value to some plants if they are one-offs. The irreplaceable are permitted to be ugly for a considerable length of time to allow them the chance to prove they have no credible potential to be pretty for me or anyone else.

Yet more times than not, my ability to look beyond what truly needs to be executed—literally—is simple laziness on my part. When taking possession of Windcliff, we inherited the tam juniper (*Juniperus sabina* 'Tamariscifolia') that Peg and Mary had devoted a considerable amount of prime real estate to around the existing house. It is to a plantsman what a stick of margarine might have been to Julia Child.

It was a substantial time after reconstruction of the house that I at last coveted this prominent expanse of full sun directly below our terrace for something that offered more than a shag of annoyingly sharp blue-gray foliage. Anyone who has removed even a small specimen of any juniper knows precisely why my procrastination had been so devout. It was wretched work, resulting in a significant loss of blood and a pile of debris roughly the size of Rhode Island.

The downside of any deliberate rehash in the garden is, of course, that you are left with the embarrassment of a new beginning. The tam juniper, in its infinite boredom, had at least provided a patina of age to the space (plus about four hundred square feet that required neither weeding nor water). Three years later, the makeover has recovered. *From four-inch pots.* I am shouting here to get your attention. Beware the pitfalls of second-guessing your uncompromising decision to at last get on with it by rushing out to buy a mature, meaningless blob of nothing to fill the gap. You will have made no progress.

Editing in my garden begins after elaborate and scholarly research into the ultimate height, spread, and hardiness of those plants to be incorporated into the new space. (Insert laughing emojis here.)

Remember that scene in *Butch Cassidy and the Sundance Kid* where Robert Redford explains to Paul Newman that he doesn't want to jump off the cliff into the river to make their escape because he doesn't know how to swim? Paul Newman responds lyrically, "Hell, the jump's probably going to kill you."

This is precisely the way in which I try out new plants in the garden during the editing process. I jump in believing most of what I am including is going to die and happily embrace those that successfully swim to shore for another day. This approach, I believe, is how I have learned the most about plant hardiness, appropriateness for the site, and the plant's chances of looking good—I mean really happy—for a really long time.

A white moment with *Olearia ×olei-folia* 'Waikariensis', *Leptospermum scoparium*, and *Nassella tenuissima* illustrates that Windcliff began as any garden will—with the gardener learning which plants respond to the soil, light, and water he has and letting them guide him to explore the like-minded.

Ultimately, okay . . . *probably* I will discover that my spacing was ill thought out or that the textural contrast I was hoping for was not sufficient, or the plant became too tall. I am on my eighth iteration of searching for the perfect plant to grow on the southeast corner outside our kitchen; we look out on it from the breakfast nook with the warmth of the AGA stove nearby. Seven times in fifteen years, I have begun again here. Six times I have lamented my choice, obliterated the view, or wasted a lot of effort (have we even talked about credit card limits yet?) with plants I had somewhat carefully considered long-term candidates. *Arctostaphylos manzanita* 'Mt Hood'. Gone. *Clianthus puniceus*. Really dead. *Cestrum nocturnum*. Sincerely dead. The space has now been occupied by *Grevillea lavandulacea* 'Penola' for three months. So far, so good. In my capriciousness, however, I have added several plants to my repertoire of what to grow, or not, again.

Once armed with knowledge of what a plant can do for me, if it's going to do for me, I can move it anywhere. And if it doesn't do, I can give it to Shayne Chandler, a most excellent friend and traveling companion. Shayne will take anything. Don't be a-shayned to give your underperformers to good friends with whom you share a friendly gardening competition. At least your garden will look the better for it.

By now, those from climates far different from the Pacific Northwest are rolling their eyes while reading my self-pitying comments from a hardiness zone that might seem like nirvana to most. As a matter of fact, our climate is as sincere as Cruella de Vil. With her long cigarette holder in hand, she invites, cajoles, and encourages for a decade or longer until, after missing a dose of Zyprexa, she screams with vindictive laughter for seventy-two hours. Three days every decade can determine what we can successfully cultivate. Cruella, that callous puppy-abusing control freak, makes the editing decisions for you, and you despise her for it. Yet how easily one is again deceived by her charms when she's back on her meds.

I ruminate on the gardening process as a set of open spiral stairs. Wherever we are on the staircase, we can look up to people who know more than us, and we can look back to see those who are now where we once were. We are continually climbing and getting better at what we do in this astonishing, maddening craft. Cognizant of those above us, we are thankful to be coaxed to take the next step higher. In theory, the people down the rung shouldn't have to make the same mistakes I have.

Those above me (there are multitudes) will shoot glances of contempt or chuckle among themselves as I offer those slightly downslope these few encouraging words: texture and foliage, height and movement, seasonality, fragrance, balance and repetition.

Texture and Foliage

WE ARE ALL TOO EAGER to equate flowers and gardens, a point brought home to me during my frequent travels about the country to speak on gardening. In the forced conversations I often find myself part of, the audience most commonly thinks in terms of blossom. If shown any plant with even the most sensational leaf form or pattern, they ask me the same question: "What does it do?" I am often moved to reply, "Well, what do you do?"

The perfection of each flower and its associated natural history can indeed dazzle the novice as layer on layer of mystery is revealed. Yet what I have come to embrace in my middle earth of gardening is the same reverence for the leaf. Its individual shape and color, its edge and petiole, its carriage and texture are the end results of its faultless voyage to survival and procreation. There is certainly enough entertainment in four billion years of design to occupy my

ABOVE · The master of editing in the garden remains our climate, which can coddle us for a decade, then lash out, determining what we can and cannot grow.

OPPOSITE TOP · *Hakonechloa macra* 'Aureola' and *Taxus baccata* 'Aureovariegata' light the path from the driveway along the east side of the house to the bluff and lower entrance to the house.

OPPOSITE BOTTOM · *Gunnera tinctoria*, collected as seed in Chile in 1998, responds well to a blast of full sun as long as its feet remain happily moist, as they do on the lower southeast slope of the bluff.

senses and encourage a greater appreciation of this simply marvelous platform of photosynthesis.

This concept is no revelation to those who have recognized the strength of foliage in the garden. I am not forging new territory here. Yet, for the freshman gardener, there seems to be no coercion or simple pleading that will force a retreat from floral flirtation. Christopher Lloyd once said, "It is an indisputable fact that appreciation of foliage comes at a late stage in our education. It is undoubtedly an acquired taste, one that grows on us."

Nurseries, blossom dens pushing floral addictions and thwarting the quantum leap to foliage, don't exactly make it easy. Weekly congregations of featured color spots annihilate the sensibilities of even those most secure in their convictions of Foliage First.

We can entrust our gardens to the strength of foliage in numerous ways. Scenes of leaf upon leaf are undoubtedly the most lasting compositions.

Along the drive, a congregation of mostly evergreen shrubs and grasses provides year-round effects, and in autumn, the orange-red flowers of *Epilobium californica* offer floral enhancement.

OPPOSITE · The color maze of South Africa in spring would be lifeless in terms of textural contrast without color, while the flower-less composition of *Oplopanax*, *Streptopus*, *Iris*, *Tolmiea*, and *Veratrum* on Mount Roberts, above Juneau, Alaska, holds together as well in black and white as it does in its naturally verdant state. Boldness of leaf is less about actual size and more about the juxtaposition of differing-sized and -shaped foliage.

The use of black-and-white imagery, mindlessly easy with current technology on a desktop or smartphone, is an effortless exercise in studying existing textural contrasts in your garden. By a simple selection from a menu of possibilities in our photo programs, we can see where we have been as gardeners and where we might be heading. Silencing the distraction of color in the image provides tremendous approbation for the use of good foliage. Though perhaps more ephemeral, the use of foliage as an effective foil for flowers throughout the year represents its true strength.

It is foolish to think that we gardeners could bypass the seduction of flowers. Yet the sooner we develop an appreciation for the imperturbable disposition of

ABOVE · *Saxifraga stolonifera, Podophyllum pleianthum*, and *Asplenium scolopendrium* 'Dixter', a gift from Christopher Lloyd in the early 1990s, mingle in the office alcove.

ABOVE LEFT · The foliage of *Geranium* ×*oxonianum* 'Katherine Adele', named for Robert's endearing mother, provides a charming backdrop to flowers that are as sweet as their namesake.

foliage and recognize the shortcomings of a garden strictly devoted to floral craft, the more years of contentment await in our gardens.

Height and Movement

I WAS IN THE INFANCY of my understanding of the juxtaposition of plants when I began gardening at Heronswood. Looking at photographs I took during those formative years, mindful of the fact that at the time I believed I had reached the essence of perfection, I can now see how off the mark I was. Everywhere and everywhen, the distinguishing feature of my plantings could have been summed up as "Are you as bored as I am?"

Those first borders were as flat as a flounder, devoid of the exclamatory peaks between dips and valleys that coax our eyes out of the Barcalounger for a

A quintet of *Pittosporum tenuifolium* 'Tasman Ruffles', rising here amidst newly emerging grasses in spring, adds strong verticality on the bluff throughout the year.

Columns of *Ilex crenata*
'Sky Pencil' interrupt
the relative sameness
of height of agapanthus
and *Molinia caerulea*.

bit of ocular exercise. Without differences in height, any assemblage of plants becomes stultifying.

An early illuminating moment on the subject came from an educational display of grasses I happened upon at Kew Gardens near London. Though composed of many different genera squeezed together, from a distance they appeared to be one static, monstrous muddle begging to be lit afire. It was indeed an educational display, ironically from a contingent of plants that can best serve the gardener in creating height differential.

Visiting artist Marcia Donahue's paranormic, dreamlike garden in Berkeley, California, when I was younger also had an enormous impact on my understanding that we own the airspace above our gardens to the degree that the FAA allows. Marcia the Magician dazzled me dizzy by utilizing her creativity with trees to grab my head and point it upward.

So I learned. The introduction of vertical elements has become important to me. The erupting, interrupting spears of yucca, phormium, and nolina at Windcliff thrust themselves above and separate the goings-on between and below. They become the frame that contains the commotion. Fastigiate plants, generally selections from more corpulent species, are put to good use for precisely the same reason. They offer an economy of space while inserting a line that interposes the horizon.

Initially, I foolishly opted for immediacy of effect, purchasing larger specimens of a narrow version of the Alaskan yellow cedar (*Cupressus nootkatensis* 'Green Arrow'). Their upsurge from the garden soon enough became an intrusion on the sky utterly out of proportion; their rather expensive roots are still slowly decomposing in my soil.

The prayer flags we erected, though for reasons well beyond creating a visually satisfying garden, now serve the same imagistic purpose as the deceased *Cupressus*. We assembled the *Darchog* to bring increased life, health, and good fortune to all sentient creatures on Earth after first cutting down five perfectly healthy trees that were beginning to shade the garden.

Our brains employ two independent networks to balance our bodies, and we can use both to balance the garden. The movement of our eyes from one static element to another is what I just droned on about. The other, kinetic movement, has become the most important of the visual cues intercepted by eyesight and cogitated upon in my tiny little brain.

Heronswood was, generally speaking, an atmospherically quiet place to garden. Other than dodging falling Doug-fir limbs during windstorms, we gave virtually no thought to, nor garnered inspiration from, a garden that moved.

The world is a dynamic package, said Einstein. When he wrote that, I rather doubt he was contemplating the cranelike dance of the flowers of *Austroderia*

fulvida that perform at this very moment outside my window. Yet it is precisely how I have come to better understand life around me—through the salsa and tango, bop and rhumba of the plants.

Windcliff brought our experience of weather systems alive. For god's sake, the place was called Windcliff before we purchased it. I should have known that barometric chaos was in store.

I now see my garden—especially on the bluff side—as an orchestrated gambol with the westerlies as maestro. There is a mesmerizing emotional delight in watching a frond of *Trachycarpus fortunei* pulsate like a bad case of the nerves. Or the busy gentle bob of the wind-drawn *Dierama*, or the *Rhodocoma* whipping about in a passionate pirouette during a wintertime assault from the south.

It is not only the wind that plants amplify but so too the lack of air movement. If the preposterously long awns of *Stipa barbata* are ever still, I am more than certain that life is momentarily on hold, begging the question, "If there

Grasses are homegrown anemometers we can check from our windows, their shift and shuttle in wind on our bluff as portentous as their stillness in perfectly quiet air.

were no movement in the universe, would time continue to pass?" What do you think, Einstein?

Water in the garden, too, projects and attracts the interchange between the animate and inanimate. It becomes the reason those feathered electrons and protons animating the sky above come into what we have created. It casts its refractions and ripples on foliage and brings clouds to the earth, that simple molecule, a powerful tranquilizer in a pool or rill or simple vessel. In one form or another, water claps its hands and makes us aware that this is why it is.

Seasonality

HAVING BEEN BIRTHED IN A REGION with four seriously Germanic seasons, I have found it one of my greatest challenges to rethink the garden as a twelve-month continuum rather than a seasonal event. It has also been work to understand and accept that the lights will dim along the corridors between

I am utterly seduced by the elegant white poppies of *Romneya coulteri* in summer, all the while knowing their foliage and stems will do absolutely nothing for me in December.

the shifts of temperature and day length. It was Christopher Lloyd (or was it Graham Stuart Thomas?) who once said, "Take care of winter and the remainder of the seasons will take care of themselves." So true, yet advice neither generally heeded nor easily followed. A lucky man I would be if I could practice what I preach, as I am simply never satisfied with my garden in dormancy.

For a keen horticulturist, it has been said, the end of the gardening season begins with the demise of the snowdrops of mid-January. In rapid-fire succession, our perennials, shrubs, and trees reach their floral zenith and flash opulently in late winter through midsummer. This is generally the way the natural world was designed. Evolution has not sided with delaying procreation, rather with getting the whole messy affair over with as quickly as possible and making hay while the sun shines. Good enough.

The problem is, well, there is always a problem. It is an undeniably innate human response to lengthening days in early spring to stir from our dingy dens and prepare the earth for another harvest, whether comestible or visual. Prompted by the impact of increased photon levels on our reptilian brains, we flock like returning geese to the nearest nursery and fill our carts with anything that further excites our retinas. The results in our gardens are brief, uncontrolled detonations of riotous—even nauseating—color. Soon enough, the flash and sizzle of the spring garden is gone and forgotten. Our instincts then direct us to consume large quantities of watermelon and hotdogs and lather on suntan lotion.

Although my saurian brain can appreciate an occasional overdose of watermelon and hotdogs, my higher self demands that we overcome the compression of twelve months of horticultural rebirth into three weeks of chromatic discord.

A case in point: drive through any Seattle neighborhood in April and early May to experience repeated incoherent congregations of color—from rhododendrons alone—that could hold their own against any set of long nails drawn across a fresh blackboard. Perhaps credit card companies should put seasonal caps on horticultural purchases. "We regret to inform you that you have exceeded your chlorophyllic-related purchasing limits for this season. *You may again begin buying plants on June 22.*"

And then, invariably, it happens again in summer. Drunk with satisfaction from the garden's ebullience in spring and wishing to make close friends and family feel horticulturally inadequate, one plans a garden party as days lengthen and temperatures increase; enter the above-mentioned hotdogs, watermelon, and generous servings of gloat. And again, without fail, the garden stumbles a week prior to the gathering, obliging a pathetic and wistful reminiscence of what your guests might have seen.

DESIGN PRINCIPLES

Kniphofia drepano-phylla blossoms in early November amidst late airy flowers of *Panicum virgatum*.

Whereas even the best-planned garden will have surges and retreats, integration of dependable bridge plants that seamlessly suture the seasons one to another will at least add to the illusion of a garden that never ceases to intimidate. But this, of course, is where I begin to cross the line in telling people how it is and when it is that they should enjoy their gardens. I am sensitive to that hubris. It is just that, well, it pains me to see so much improvident purchasing during early-season feeding frenzies in every garden center in America.

There is no sacrifice to any season if thought is given to foliage, silhouette, flower, fruit, and bark. Nor is there a magic ratio of plants performing in spring or autumn, summer or winter. It is simply a matter of visiting gardens—and nurseries—in all four seasons and rationing your plant budget. It is a matter of knowing where it is you plan on placing a plant in the garden (and we all know you know precisely where you plan on placing a plant before you purchase it) and asking these simple questions of the plant: What are you doing for me today? What will you be doing for me six months from today? Which one of your neighbors is planning on picking up the slack when you are on your coffee break?

OPPOSITE · A favorite of our winter-resident Anna's hummingbirds, *Grevillea victoriae*, from southeastern Australia, begins blossoming on the bluff in early November and continues through the winter until April, no matter what temperatures are thrown its way.

BELOW · Apparently, *Grevillea* 'Canterbury Gold' has never been told it is allowed a coffee break; it blossoms twelve months a year, more profusely in winter months.

OPPOSITE TOP · Explosive sunrises over the Cascades and sunsets over the Olympics become the primary form of entertainment during the severely truncated days of late November through early February.

OPPOSITE BOTTOM · Late summer brings ripening fruit, a welcome feast for eyes weary of a tired garden and for birds preparing for migration. *Sorbus ulleungensis*, a collection from South Korea in 1993, dependably puts on a fruitful display in the upper meadow.

Rhus typhina 'Tiger Eyes' transitions from bright yellow summer foliage to rich gamboge just as the first rains of autumn begin in late October.

LEFT · The flared flowers of *Cyclamen hederifolium*, in shades of white through deep pink, appear as the temperatures decrease in early September and then approach crescendo in mid to late October. After the plant flowers, bewitchingly good marbled and patterned leaves appear as a winter ground cover.

BELOW · Its variegated foliage having withered by early July, *Nerine bowdenii* 'Mollie Cowie' flashes flowers in an almost embarrassing shade of pink on naked stems in early November. In some unnatural fashion, it seems to consort well with foliar autumn color.

Fragrance

DIANE ACKERMAN, in her book *A Natural History of the Senses*, says it better than I ever could: "Nothing is more memorable than a smell. One scent can be unexpected, momentary and fleeting, yet conjure up a childhood summer beside a lake in the mountains." Considering the fact that it is now believed that the roughly four hundred scent receptors in the human brain can work in concert to distinguish one trillion odors, there is plenty of room in a gardener's mind for fragrance-associated memories.

During my first winter in Seattle, living in the Stone Cottage in Washington Park Arboretum, I first detected the overwhelming perfume of the winter box, *Sarcococca confusa*, at roughly the same time I became aware that I was developing the horrific influenza that was making the rounds. The fragrance from this genus still takes me back to that miserable week, but fortuitously I have layered upon it more pleasant memories that help break the high fever.

Blame my age-defeated retinas, the neuropathy in my digits, or my sensorineural hearing loss if you must consider a cause, but it is the instrumentality of fragrance that has surged to lead the pack for me when I am selecting, and especially placing, plants at Windcliff. If I ever had a trillion memories, I am too old to remember a fraction, but my cache of smells will keep me wined and dined for all of my remaining days.

The windward side of the house is particularly important, as it is from Puget Sound that the air moves toward the house and carries the aura of foliage and flower. Planted there, *Escallonia illinita* barely possesses enough visual ornament to allow it the considerable space its girth occupies. But in the depths of winter or in summer, without warning or the necessity of proximity to the shrub, delicious bombs of curry detonate to a degree that makes visitors wonder what's cooking on the AGA stove.

I keep *Spartium junceum* growing directly on the bluff edge, as the North African thrives on poor soil and neglect. Its pervasive sweet vanilla-like perfume lifts across the garden, into and over the house and onward to the leeside. Its vexatious yellow, like that of Scotch broom, is forgiven.

Rosemary is grown near the kitchen terrace for obvious reasons. In winter or summer, it too releases its scent to combine with other fragrances hovering nearby to make unique bouquets. Its aroma is particularly good with that of the intensely coconut-oil-scented flowers of *Olearia* ×*oleifolia* 'Waikariensis'. I count the fragrance of this daisy bush as only one of its many fine attributes, including handsome gray evergreen foliage, a polite size, and a propensity to self-cleanse after flowering. Numerous other specimens of *Olearia* are included throughout the garden, but none are as fragrant as this.

Magnolia wilsonii, one of the few magnolias with flowers that hang gracefully downward, smells sweetly of lily of the valley.

The fragrance of
Spartium junceum
carries from the bluff
throughout the garden.

As much as I would have hoped otherwise, Windcliff grows a lousy lavender, probably resulting from soils that are too moisture retentive in the winter. I love its fragrance and would have probably overused it to a cliché had I been permitted. Gardenias, too, despite such reassuring names as 'Kleim's Hardy' and 'Frostproof', deprive me of what I consider to be the Queen Mother of all fragrances. The plants actually go into decline on the trip back home from the nursery and never recover. Yearning denied.

Directly outside the dining room on the windward side I have planted *Datura meteloides*, related to, but hardier than, *Brugmansia*. The same species was planted around the patio of my parents' home in Evart, opening its swooningly fragrant, pendulous white blossoms in early evening, summoning sphinx moths to its nectar. Adjacent to the datura on our terrace grows *Impatiens tinctoria*, a surprisingly hardy East African species from high elevations on Mount Kenya, with broad, purple-throated white flowers that become olfactorily active after sunset.

Nearby, squeezed between the two plants just mentioned, is *Philadelphus madrensis*, a mock orange from the Southwest extending into Mexico. I refuse

Podophyllum pleianthum has an earthy fragrance attractive to flies for pollination.

ABOVE · *Impatiens tinctoria*, from Mount Kenya but perfectly hardy in the ground, pulses at dusk and has been deliberately used near the door of our dining room.

ABOVE RIGHT · The minty fresh fragrance of *Prostanthera cuneata* 'Badja Peak' engulfs the air on summer and winter days alike, not from the flowers but the foliage.

to say whether this might be responsible for my Claritin abuse during its blossoming season, as its inimitable grape-jelly scent is simply too phenomenal to blame for anything, including an overactive autoimmune response.

Along the drive I have planted things designed for an overachieving horticulturist who takes only the time to lower the windows in passing at peak moments of the year to engage with their chemical inventories, which, in turn, engage with clusters of cells within my dual intake valves. *Edgeworthia chrysantha*, collected in northeast Sichuan. *Hydrangea angustipetala*, collected in Taiwan. *Magnolia wilsonii*, collected in Yunnan. *Sarcococca wallichiana*, collected in eastern Nepal. *Mahonia tikushiensis*, from Taiwan.

Also growing near the drive, but not too closely, is the *Philadelphus* or mock orange that I helped my mom transplant from her father's garden to our own in Evart. It is, as I write this, in full blossom and causing me significant sinusitis discomfort, but not enough to ever consider disrespecting the mille-feuille confection brought to life by its esters pulsed into the air.

Forced to slow to the car's dumb-dog speed of 1.5 mph, with windows fully down and a reasonable ambient air temperature, I'm smacked silly by muffled memories exploding in my sinonasal cavities.

Balance and Repetition

ACHIEVING BALANCE IN THE GARDEN is a concept more easily sensed, I think, by blurring your vision—a freshly cut onion will do it—and feeling the weight of mass and color across a space. Windcliff provided me with this enigma that I had not fully considered before. There are certain vantages

The repetition of palms in the bluff garden stabilizes their weight while *Rosa chinensis* 'Mutabilis' blossoms nonstop throughout summer.

The very same Japanese maple that Robert and I came to prune at Windcliff two decades before purchasing the property is still here, visually communicating with cyclamen in autumn along with *Hydrangea aspera* Villosa Group, collected on my first trip to Yunnan in 1996.

from our house and terrace where I can feel, if not see, the entirety of the bluff. Attempting to describe how and why I feel something is askew slips into the realm of feng shui, which interestingly enough translates literally from the Chinese into "wind water." Though I know I will certainly offend the many believers in the "invisible forces," I have interacted with enough feng shui masters to know that one man's yin is another's yang. Balance in the garden changes daily and seasonally, as it should. Explaining the wants of more of this and less of that, however, begins to reveal a person who is himself unbalanced.

Balance in the realm of gardening is first cousin to repetition, which was the means of cohering any garden space that I attempted to hone at Heronswood. Cyclical repetitions of color, shape, and mass do indeed initiate movement of the eye from one correspondent to the next. I would hire a repetition master (or read Val Easton's *A Pattern Garden*) long before I'd commission a feng shui practitioner. Does this make sense, or am I repeating myself?

Balance can shift significantly from season to season. In spring, the acid greens of emerging foliage and the blistering yellows of *Spartium*, *Adenocarpus*,

The similar mounding habits of *Cistus*, *Olearia*, *Grevillea*, and *Cortaderia* lead the eye across the bluff.

Genista, and *Cassia* jump to the fore and organize my eyes while driving mad the visitors to the garden who possess the all-too-prevalent aversion to this color. Then come the pinks and purples of *Lavatera* and *Dierama*, bonding nicely with creams and golds from the grasses. Later in summer, the composition becomes heavily skewed to blue with *Agapanthus*; though the genus projects a wide spectrum within this primary color, my eyes and brain easily do the work required to hold it together.

Agapanthus repeats throughout the garden from midsummer to early autumn.

Rite to Privacy

Call me a misanthrope, but I do not like to garden (or eat) (or bathe) under the curious gaze of the folks next door. I don't believe myself to be alone. Though some people prefer, indeed consider it an ordained right, to share common visual ground with their neighbors, the need to interact with the outside world takes a nosedive for many people I know when ensconced in their own home and garden.

When we first arrived on the property, we possessed an agoraphobic expanse of mown turf and an endless horizon. We also purchased next-door neighbors who had built their home inches within code of our eastern boundary line. Having lived at Heronswood for two decades with no neighbors, we felt unnerved at the sense of being observed. Additionally, the house next door was big. And yellow. There was a young child who made pathetic sounds on her coronet, which made the house even yellower. Something had to be done.

We eucalyptized the house. Anyone who has grown any eucalyptus knows you can easily achieve ten feet from a seedling within twelve hours. I planted *Eucalyptus neglecta*, one of the hardiest of the genus, and handsome, with large smoky blue foliage. From a four-inch pot it vaulted to thirty feet tall and as broad in just three years. Yet I knew then I was not planting the permanent screening we ultimately needed.

The eucalyptus was sited significantly forward in the line of vision, which meant it would take less time to do its intended business (a ten-foot tree close to you does the work of a fifty-foot tree in the distance). Behind it and directly along the property line we planted the slower-growing tapestry that is in place today: ×*Cuprocyparis leylandii* 'Golconda', *Cryptomeria japonica* 'Gyokuryu', *Azara microphylla*, *Osmanthus delavayi*, and *Acacia pravissima*. The plants were composed in a well-ordered descent in height from tallest (near the yellow house) to lowest (toward the bluff edge). I wanted to disappear our neighbors without destroying their view.

It became a matter of great satisfaction while using our council ring to deliberately look for that looming yellow structure and not see a trace of it. We could still hear the coronet. She

surely did not major in music when she left home for college a few years later.

The very month we moved into our new home in 2004, the fully unexpected happened. Construction began on what had been a blessedly empty piece of land on our western boundary. We endured the construction of an imposing chalet painted in tones that vibrated much like a badly played instrument. Perhaps most oddly, the neighbor's kitchen deck was oriented to peer down directly into our master bedroom suite and outdoor shower.

The suturing of the bluff plantings to the immediacy of the house was well under way when we realized our new neighbors' intent. Our response was to surround the entire western side of the house with a mountainous pile of soil. Capping the berm with a few expensive, specimen-sized *Cedrus deodara* and *Picea orientalis*, we thought the chapter of privacy making at Windcliff was written.

Then came the construction of their garage, bringing out the serious firepower. The structure was so enormous and ungainly that we began referring to it as the barrage. In response, we staggered big bamboo—*Phyllostachys dulcis*, *P. bambusoides* 'Castillonis', *P. nigra*, *P. glauca* 'Yunzhu', *Chusquea gigantea*, and *Fargesia robusta*—along the western edge of the property. A structure without a modicum of grace in a proportion fit for giraffe breeding was bamboozled virtually overnight.

The screening settled in, as did we. By complete serendipity, in the process of liberating ourselves from the visual clutter next door, we had created a bamboo allée. It remains to this day one of the most tranquil strolls in the garden. Disappointingly, as of 2019, two of the bamboo species—*Phyllostachys glauca* 'Yunzhu' and *P. bambusoides* 'Castillonis'—have commenced their flowering sequence and will soon enough be only memories. No matter, as the original neighbors have been replaced by fine gardeners, one of whom is very good on the guitar.

Using bamboo to screen the property to the west created an enchanting path from the drive to the bluff.

OPPOSITE Screening the property lines became important upon acquiring the land. We used eucalyptus in the distance and foreground for immediate effect. Within five years of planting, the long-term conifers were taking control of the situation, allowing us to regain garden territory by removing the eucalyptus.

DESIGN PRINCIPLES

The
Bluff

An aerial photo of the bluff illuminates the density of planting while revealing the positions of the upper fire pit, portions of the water features, and the bluffside council ring.

Now, nineteen years on, we have jettisoned the panoramic affluence from most of the living quarters. This confuses a number of our friends, many of them designers for whom we have great respect. I once wrote that if you have to work just a bit to savor a beautiful view, it makes the view more beautiful. I believe those were my original thoughts, but if they were paraphrased from someone I read, my apologies. They are true words nonetheless.

My View from the Kitchen Table

WE REMAIN BEACONED OUTSIDE not only visually but also acoustically. On the precise moment I sat to write this on an early Sunday morning of perfection in July, we were called to the bluff edge by the echoing chants of the S'Klallam, Suquamish, Nisqually, Duwamish, Tulalip, Skagit, and other Lushootseed tribal canoes on their annual journey from one tribal land to the next.

Often a fledgling bald eagle finds purchase in our bluffside madronas or grand firs and incessantly and irritatingly shrieks and screeches for a meal delivered by airfreight. After an hour or so of tolerating these complaints, I will often go to the base of its perch and attempt to explain to it the long-established rules of weaning and flight development for its species and that it must now buck up and fish or cut bait. The eaglet generally pays no attention.

Visually. Outside the kitchen window are the fingerlike fronds of the Mediterranean fan palm, *Chamaerops humilis*, a low, multistemmed species from southern Europe and North Africa. I like what it does with its leaves in the wind, especially in winter, vibrating like the white-gloved hands of Jack Nicholson overacting in *Batman*.

From this vantage, the digits of this palm seemingly hold aloft the outside bird feeder. With an ample garden replacing the bleached sterility of lawn, our bird population has erupted to biblical proportions, if indeed bird populations come in that size. It is, in short, staggering. On the feeder at this moment are, starting from the left, a black-headed grosbeak; jumping to the far right, a hairy woodpecker; and crowning the top, an outlandish number of band-tailed pigeons the size of large vultures vying for purchase. This congregation of birds momentarily pauses and quiets itself as a slicing shadow passes across the landscape. I have come to recognize this governing, gliding shade as that of a mature bald eagle sailing toward its aerie just to the east of our house.

Rotating slightly to the right, out of view unless I stand, a self-sown seedling of *Ceanothus* 'Dark Star' has concocted an absurdly blue moment. This is a surreal hue, sucking dry the blue of the sky and sea in one breath when in full blossom. I was initially taken with the genus and planted a sizeable collection of species and cultivars. One by one, they were snuffed out by harsh or overly wet winters and proved to be downright mean in their death when we sliced and diced them to dispose of their remains. It is only this seedling that remains on the entirety of the bluff.

To the left, directly on the bluff edge, is an old second-growth campanile of *Abies grandis* or grand fir. Grand it is, too, enduring winter gales beyond the

The view from the dining terrace encompasses the Lutyens-inspired steps and Tahoma in the distance. From this viewpoint, I see the distraction of life and form in every direction that we gardeners strive to invite into our landscapes and, too often, do not pause long enough to marvel over.

call of duty and, with only half a foothold, remaining resolute. This champion is answered on the right by a maturing grove of madrona, *Arbutus menziesii*, growing in its precise niche on a seaside edge and, in so doing, preserving the integrity of our escarpment.

I must move now, coffee in hand, to the terrace; it is especially inviting on a sunny summer's morning. Between the grand fir and the madrona I see an extended lay of jabbled water with facets dashing the brilliance of the sun in a fulgurant dance of light. This avenue of diamonds narrows, leading to the mother of volcanoes, Tahoma, commonly known as Mount Rainier, rising glacier-clad to two miles above the skyline of Seattle.

After nearly two decades, the bluff we first walked upon as our very own in the early summer of 2000 is no longer that vast space that pulsed with heat and infertility even on a cloudy day. The area of mown turf—which was actually cut on a weekly basis six months out of the year—was at that time overpowering in possibilities but intimidating in scale. Its capaciousness has shrunk, much in the way a large interior space might be reduced by oversized furniture. We have lost a chunk or two to the sound by slides during winter rains, but nothing significant as yet. And, yes, the terrace and its adjoining water features have pressed considerably into its expansiveness. It remains the plants, in scale and quantity, that have made more intimate an exposed and open pitch that had previously provoked bouts of agoraphobia.

Planting: Fights, Camera, Action

AS I BEGAN MAKING MY NEW GARDEN atop this blustery bluff precariously balanced above Puget Sound, I initiated the exploration of a flora mostly unknown to me. I chose plants with differing textures and heights, as well as those that would provide fragrance from time to time and movement in the landscape throughout the year. Plants that could tolerate the pauperized soil condition of glacial till, along with strong winds, cold winter temperatures, and a limited amount of rainfall during the growing season. To paraphrase longtime friend and horticulturist Lauren Springer, who has outshone the lot of us in gardening in hostile environments, I began to hurl every four-inch potted plant I believed might have the prospect of success at this not-yet-understood canvas to see what might stick. Many did not.

I did not then, nor would I now, possess the acumen to plant an amply sized football field in one go. Developing the space by dividing and conquering over three consecutive years seemed reasonable on many levels, including maintenance after the disturbance of a monumentally sized cache of weed seeds. More important, this strategy guided me in terms of apposite plant selection going forward as one year informed the next. It remains one of the few times in my life that I have approached anything resembling rationality.

On the first summer's day when temperatures rose above 70 degrees F, I began spraying the turf of the initial planting area with undiluted white vinegar. By nightfall, what had been green that morning was sincerely toasted. The vinegar did not kill the deep-rooted perennial weeds, many of which had existed here, seemingly, prior to the last glacial epoch. These were dispensed with by hand or spot treated with a systemic herbicide.

Wishing no injury to the Salish Sea by runoff during the first rains of autumn and selfishly wanting to retain as much topsoil as possible, I neither tilled nor amended the soil in its entirety before planting, believing the knit of the existing slowly decaying turf—left quite unmolested between plantings— would stabilize the site until my chosen subjects took command of the situation. In that assumption, I was proven correct.

TOP · Phase one of planting the bluff commenced in 2001 with *Embothrium coccineum* and *Cortaderia selloana*, both seed collections from Chile in 1998, planted directly into the vanquished turf without tilling.

BOTTOM · Divisions of the existing colonies of *Agapanthus praecox* growing at Windcliff bask in sunshine on the bluff.

In what may have seemed like an exercise in futility to many, I began placing ridiculously small plants or fresh divisions in generously proportioned individual holes. To correct deficiencies in major nutrients, I placed slow-release fertilizer at the bottom of each hole and topped it with a toupee of removed sod to prevent possible runoff of nutrients to the waters below. Plants were placed and the remaining space was backfilled with existing soil—that is, rocks with a dash of sand for good measure.

Penny wise but pound foolish, after planting I grasped anything at my avail for mulch to preserve moisture and suppress weeds jubilant at being provided a welcoming environment. The resulting collage of differing materials meant to encourage the establishment of plants too diminutive to perceive at thirty paces made for countless quiet dinners at our table as Robert cogitated on the

transformation of our bluff from a scene of green compose to that of a midcentury trailer park. Comments might have included some encouraging consideration of tires planted up with red pelargoniums and pink flamingos. I've put these conversations entirely out of my mind.

For three years, each year armed with a greater understanding of which plants were going to not simply endure but thrive, I repeated the process, while sustaining the plants I had already established. By the end of the growing season in 2003, trialing of plants and evaluation of their performance on the bluff was in high gear, while full screening of the adjoining property was within reach.

I offer here a valuable lesson learned in the process to anyone making a garden in a comparable fashion. Taking the time to look toward the next phase before you actually arrive with all guns pulled, and establishing the slower-growing structural plants a year or two before, will bring a greater degree of immediate gratification upon tackling the space in earnest. It also instigates a more lively and loving conversation at the dinner table.

There were losses, of course. No dearth of death on my bluff. Big surprise . . . *drum roll* . . . I spaced my four-inch pots too closely. Even bigger surprise . . . *cymbal crash* . . . I still do to this day. And with planting well under way, I

By the end of the growing season in 2003, full screening of the adjoining property was within reach. *Molinia caerulea* 'Skyracer', the bleached stems in this early photograph, proved too tall for its selected position and was moved farther to the bluff side. *Chondropetalum tectorum* ultimately proved too sissified for our climate, and the lavenders refused to survive.

realized that I wasn't paying attention to framing views as much as I should have been. I was still gardening foot by foot as I had at Heronswood rather than peering through the garden to the lambent waters beyond.

To assuage my failures, we opened a series of view corridors focusing the eye somewhither beyond. ("Admiration points" these would have been called by Sibylle Kreutzberger and Pamela Schwerdt, the two remarkable women who gardened for Vita Sackville-West at Sissinghurst Castle for decades. They had visited Windcliff during their last speaking tour of North America and suggested this nomenclature in my nascent garden as I struggled with its design.) We did this without contouring the land, instead employing a differential in plant height—low-growing plants flanked by those taller—while creating a false perspective by siting the farthest framing plants closer together than those to the fore. After we made numerous attempts, the visual pathways have become successful, at least in regard to providing a resting point that begs one to pause and consider for a moment the composition of the planting and the endpoint to which the eye is drawn.

On Garden Maintenance

I HAVE ALWAYS COMPARED WEEDING to paying on the principal. For each weed removed before seed dispersal, you have less interest to pay on the loan—or is that, play on the loam? Helen Dillon says it best in her superb book *Garden Artistry*: "The lazier you are, the more diligently you should weed, for each weed taken out before it sets seed allows a few more minutes' lazing time."

Others, who believe weeding is a nuisance, think differently. I am always surprised when visitors to the garden ask how many people it takes to weed the place. They call my garden "the place," which sounds like a pool hall that smells of cigarettes and stale beer. They are, it seems, intimidated by the general weedlessness of the garden, either that or by the perceived profound waste of time it takes for someone to keep "the place" mostly weed-free.

Sometimes people find a weed, a tall one, and bring it to me smugly, as if they had found a fly in the ointment. I don't mind. I do not and cannot maintain "the place" on my own. I still work full-time at Heronswood, gladly so, and will volunteer weekly when my tenure as director there comes to an end. And I believe in exploring the astonishments of living outside of our garden gate, hiking, biking, or a long walk with the dogs on Sunday morning after reading the *Times*. My garden can accept a few weeds and I will not be the poorer for it.

But still I love to weed. When else can you afford the luxury of spending so much time on your hands and knees with your face nearly buried in plants?

Not all "weeds" are controlled. *Dierama, Canna indica, Verbena bonariensis,* and a few grass species are allowed to migrate throughout the bluff to sites of their own liking. We edit only when necessary.

How can you not learn from seeing the garden from such a vantage, the comings and goings of all of those things we so frequently walk by and ignore? What other job in the garden delivers such a primal instinct to kill, followed by such joy and satisfaction after the deed? You are not belaboring plant placement, or if it is or is not the right season, or second-guessing the layout of a path system. The weeds you are slaying are not criminal—in fact, they are natural perfection at its worst. Let them be not evil in someone else's garden.

I am profoundly fortunate to have Eduardo Montes as my avatar two days per week. He is a remarkable young man possessing a work ethic uncommonly encountered, especially in the world of the privileged shrimpy-whimpy white boy attempting to close the door on immigration after receiving a mail-order bride from abroad. I have also been blessed with occasional generously spirited volunteers who help me tidy up before benefit events. And I could not do the garden without Robert, who coordinates so much of the work after my abrupt departures to my job, or often for weeks away exploring for plants in the field.

Traveler's joy (*Clematis vitalba*), fireweed (*Epilobium* spp.), and butterfly bush (*Buddleia davidii*) arrive steadily by an under-radar aerial assault (mostly from Bainbridge Island, as the current of air shifts to onshore in the afternoon), while fruited species are delivered indiscriminately via payload from the unfastened bowels of birds. Though I am reluctant to seem paranoid, others must arrive by pure malevolence in the pockets of visitors whom I have somehow insulted in a former life—or perhaps last week in this life. It is a given that no matter how insistent we are in getting in the last word, we know we never will. On weeding, I leave it to the words of Mark Twain: "Continuous improvement is better than delayed perfection."

Together, Eduardo and I heavily mulch as much of the garden as I can afford, performing the task throughout the year (okay, Eduardo does most of the heavy lifting). We spread a four-inch coating of dollar bills upon our acreage, knowing that what does not blow away to the gardens of my adjoining neighbors will pay dividends in retaining soil moisture in the summer and suppress—if only for a while—the annual blitzkrieg of villainous plant species.

Though we are aware that mulch doesn't offer much in the way of fertility, we believe that by not cutting the plants back or by not clearing the debris too quickly in autumn, we increase the bioactivity of the soil. If a shovel of soil reveals an earthworm or three, I think we're doing something right.

The Proteaceae (*Telopea*, *Embothrium*, *Grevillea*, and *Banksia*) may protest any fertilizer containing phosphorus; this, along with our concern for runoff into the Salish Sea below, means a general spring broadcast is avoided. A small

handful of well-balanced fertilizer is incorporated into the hole during planting for everything other than the aforementioned proteids. Thenceforth, the general approach is to fertilize only individual plants that show folial deficiencies, lack of vigor, or limb dieback—the latter an indicator of nutrient neediness learned from Maestro Ron Determann of the Atlanta Botanical Garden.

We burn the grasses on humid, cool, and still days in February or early March; almost immediately, points of green begin to appear through the charred remains. However, as seductive as they may be for a pyromaniac, the towering stands of *Miscanthus* are not candidates for burning and instead are cut to the ground using a battery-operated hedge trimmer, the best tool invented since the goat for efficiently cutting back a plethora of perennials or reducing the size of shrubs. It seems like it would be equally effective in trimming our doodles' coats in summer, yet Robert refuses to let me try.

Pruning has no season in particular, but I am reticent to cut anything back hard after early August. Summer is especially timely for removing suckers, water sprouts, deadwood, and crossing branches, while late winter provides the opportunity to seriously attack the hydrangeas and reproportion the garden. One must keep the administration of the pruning saw in perspective. You don't have to prune. After all, the plant kingdom has been doing particularly well for itself without our intervention for 3.5 billion years, give or take a few million. But if you must, remember it is not brain surgery. You will not go to prison for bad pruning. Still, a full day of pruning with the appropriate weapons of choice on a quiet day in March remains for me a slice of heaven.

Don't hate us for not having deer. We are fenced to six feet and open to the bluff; we realize that if the deer population in our immediate vicinity were higher, the fence would provide little in the way of deterrence. I have at last admitted this in writing, and tonight the gods that monitor such things will send forth a plague on four legs, with dreamy brown eyes, to obliterate our Eden.

Our greatest suffering comes mostly from introduced species of slugs and snails; one's slimy and one's snot. (I have waited for years to use this childish line in a book.) Their control, like that of weeds, is about persistence and not about overreacting after the fact. We find that by applying Sluggo (iron phosphate, a formulation benign to birds and mammalian pets) on a regular basis beginning in late January, we can keep the populations truncated. On rare occasions, when the numbers are out of control, we will use a discriminate amount of Deadline (metaldehyde), finding that the liquid formulation has less chance than the pelleted of being carried away, especially if applied to the daytime redoubts of these destructive life forms. For the record, I have a great fondness for our native banana slug (*Ariolimax columbianus*), which in all my years of gardening has never been found guilty of disfiguring anything in my gardens.

Telopea truncata, from Tasmania, blossoms dependably in our garden though will show resetment of fertilizer with phosphorus.

Those we find here, we relocate across our lane to their chosen habitat of forest to avoid poisoning them inadvertently.

Chipmunks and rabbits are our mammalian tormentors. The former have found excellent habitat for nesting in the gabion wall we have constructed around the potager. With the wall, we have encouraged a large population that will eagerly devour an entire row of emerging peas, beans, or beets overnight. Populations of the latter ebb and flow with the health and prevalence of our native coyote population, which is low at the time of this writing due to a severe outbreak of mange. Weasels will dispatch both, and rare daytime sightings of this secretive predator are satisfyingly not uncommon. Live traps are frequently employed, and we release our catch on Bainbridge Island in exchange for the seeds of fireweed and traveler's joy they send us, or at the entrance to a garden whose owner has recently gotten on my nerves. Though we take no pleasure in the methodology, one of our doodles, Babu, is fond of rare rabbit, remitting in our face a certain circle-of-life sort of thing.

From day to day and season to season, the enigmas of maintaining the garden will prevail, continuing to be a burden and annoyance when time is ample, and blissful when I'm strapped for time and wish for nothing more than a long afternoon on my knees committing murder and mayhem on innocent inchlings.

Babu, meaning "little brother" in Nepalese, standing next to Henri, takes a break from rabbit control.

Structural Engineering

IN ANY TEMPERATE CLIMATE, no matter how forgiving or severe, it remains seductively simple to create a garden without lasting power during the off-season. Above all else, put your furniture in place before worrying over the doilies on the table. And yes, before you protest, I realize this fact. Our climate allows the use of an enumeration of broad-leaved evergreens. Stop your whining. If you must, employ fence posts for your scaffolding. Just plant them and surveil the prize.

Palm trees have always possessed considerable appeal for northern temperate gardeners, for various reasons. Of course, high on that list is their ability

Narrow columns of *Pittosporum tenuifolium* 'Tasman Ruffles' and repetition of similarly shaped foliage delivered by different species of palm hold the bluff garden together visually throughout the year. Especially important are the upright spears of *Phormium tenax*, collected by seed on the Chatham Islands in New Zealand in 2010. It is a particularly robust and hardy form of this species.

to cerebrally transport us to Margaritaville even when we are beleaguered by our somewhat-less-than-tropical winters. (It is noted that for the same reason, many gardeners find them quite inappropriate for our region.) Yet I was seeking to evoke an oasis on our bluff. The ease with which I could cultivate them, as well as the gallant texture and quivering movement their evergreen leaves lend to the garden throughout the year, was reason enough for their consideration. Not everyone feels the same; too bad for them.

The windmill palm, *Trachycarpus fortunei,* is native to mountainous regions of western China, but due to its long and multitalented utilization in human culture, the exact origin of this as well as many other palm species is often difficult to pinpoint. Immense, long-fingered leaves to three feet in width are produced throughout the year (though growth is barely noticeable during the winter) atop thick trunks ultimately rising to forty feet. Being a monocot, related to bamboo and grasses, the palm has a trunk that does not possess a cambium layer and hence has no ability to increase in girth as the plant ages. The diameter of a palm trunk when the plant is two feet tall will be, more or less, the same diameter as when it is a hundred feet tall. As the crown of palm foliage rises higher on our bluff, more of the view is once again

Slip inside the eye of your mind

Don't you know you might find a better place to play

—OASIS, "DON'T LOOK BACK IN ANGER"

Trachycarpus princeps offers movement to the bluff with delectable, broad, white-backed fronds. Too infrequently seen in gardens, this palm is native to southwestern China, where it grows on vertical limestone cliffs.

revealed while the trunk remains only a narrow exclamatory line that inter-rupts the space.

The palms—including the just-mentioned *Trachycarpus fortunei*, along with *T. fortunei* 'Wagnerianus', *T. princeps*, *Chamaerops humilis*, *Butia capitata*, *Brahea moorei*, and the very-slow-growing *Sabal minor*—were among the ini-tial major players planted on the bluff that helped to lend cohesiveness to the youthful space. All of these but the *Brahea* specimen have consistently flow-ered, offering a shout-out to yellow in summer and, on the female specimens of Trachycarpus, interesting crops of fruit. And, no, none of these arrived as small plants except the *Sabal* palms and a seedling of *T. fortunei* that I raised from the Mattituck, New York, Landcraft Environments garden of good friends Dennis Schrader and Bill Smith. The palms represented a serious investment. All, that is, but the maturing *Chamaerops humilis* specimen planted outside our kitchen door that I found for free, curbside on Shore Drive in Indianola. Lutherans love free palms.

Nolina longifolia, an arborescent or trunked species, erupts from the crown with broad, deep green leaves that pour out of a central vortex and spill gracefully downward.

That first year in my new garden presented a very steep learning curve. Accustomed to a landscape of shade, I was in shock and awe from a blustery site in blistering full sun and was in desperate need of good scaffolding. While visiting my fledgling garden for the first time, my friend Linda Cochran, a celebrated and adventurous gardener then on Bainbridge Island, suggested I try the razor grasses, as from her vantage the conditions seemed perfect. I knowingly nodded in agreement while attempting to not betray the fact that I had never once heard of razor grasses *or* the genus *Nolina*. Linda, sensing my ignorance on the matter, kindly brought two species to me the following week; I've been hooked ever since.

Distinguished by long, narrow, evergreen leaves forming either stemmed or stemless rosettes, nolinas have leaf tips that are more approachable than those of yuccas and agaves, though their pliable leaves belie edges with extremely fine and fiercely sharp teeth. We frequently find the amputated limbs of visitors to the garden who have ventured too close. Orca food.

Unlike agaves, which blossom only once and then chuck it in, nolinas continue to grow and thrive after taking a year or two off following the struggles

Nolina nelsonii, seen here in blossom, occurs naturally in only a small area of Tamaulipas, Mexico. The plants in my garden have a beguiling blue foliage color and appear much like a very robust form of *Yucca rostrata*.

of giving birth. The flowering stems, which can thrust skyward to eight feet in a matter of days, bear either male or female flowers on separate plants in branched panicles of creamy white or yellow flowers. The red, winged capsules produced on female specimens should successful fertilization occur are striking and remain effective for an impressively long season in late summer through autumn.

So too have the yuccas found a welcome at the table for their year-round presence, summer flowers, sense of movement, durability, and drought tolerance. The genus has a special place in my heart as a gardener—I brought back in a paper bag a piece of *Yucca glauca* purchased as a souvenir in South Dakota on

Yucca flaccida 'Ivory Towers' possesses the ability to be swamped by surrounding foliage during the summer months but still produce its flower-laden panicles in late summer.

Yucca rostrata 'Sapphire Skies', a selection made by Sean Hogan and introduced through Cistus Nursery, quickly established a girthy trunk of seven feet after being planted from a gallon container in 2004. *Lobelia tupa*, from southern Chile, blossoms to the fore and right. The Mt Etna broom, *Genista aetnensis*, flowers behind the yucca.

a family vacation in the 1960s. That plant in my parents' yard, though ravaged by deer each winter, returned every spring to blossom in summer for decades. I am certain it is still there, as yuccas have a belligerent way of staying put once established.

Yucca rostrata, from western Texas and northern Mexico, has been a sensational plant for us, with striking narrow blue leaves atop a thick, scaly trunk; I trim the normally retentive foliage each winter to better display the plant's form. Like the palms, I paid big for large specimens in the garden's infancy, but, also like the palms, I needn't have squandered the dough. It is a handsome plant in its trunkless youth and quickly rises skyward. Though I am far from discontented with the look of a maturing specimen, to be perfectly honest I prefer the foliar effects while the yucca is loitering in its youth at ground level.

After *Yucca rostrata* blossoms, as mine do (somewhat infrequently, I might add), the single stem branches and three to five equally imposing stems continue their journey. When I am need of another specimen, I simply amputate one of the appendages, let it dry a few days, and then plant it directly in its permanent location.

A naturally occurring hybrid, *Yucca ×schottii* grows in a pocket of extremely lean gravel surrounding the inner workings of our water feature system of pumps and filters. Long, upright blue spears of narrow foliage pierce the surrounding ground covers and grasses and will quite easily assassinate or seriously maim anyone gardening too close. It is downright malicious, and I am glad I have it sequestered on a bit of island, but when the plant is in blossom in August, with erect panicles heavily laden with large white flowers typical of the genus, all is forgiven.

It was in precisely the wrong place, however, that I sited *Yucca schidigera*, also with unforgiving stilettos on quickly developing trunks. Not bad when it was simply lacerating visitors at knee level but somewhat more disquieting as it rose to confront more sensitive anatomies. It is now too large and too stunning in effect for me to even remotely consider purging it from the garden, so instead I religiously disarm the razor-sharp points of each leaf. Fifteen years on and it has yet to blossom; it's always good to have something to look forward to. And thus far, it has disfigured no one.

Plum Island, the nomenclature of the color we stained the shingles of the house—a color that we think helps the house quiet itself in our surroundings—is carried out onto the bluff by a few shrubs that ricochet the same sonorous tone.

Rather predictably, I used *Cotinus* 'Grace' and *C. coggygria* 'Royal Purple' as cutback shrubs for the purpose. I prefer the latter for its deeper color and for its less-rank growth making it resistant to breaking during summer winds.

Yucca schidigera, the Mojave yucca, center, is now dangerously eye-level along a path well traveled by dogs and humans alike. Its leaf tips are trimmed like fingernails on a regular basis.

The shrubs are coppiced, or cut back, to two feet high in late winter, sacrificing summer bloom but forcing a more dramatic show of foliage during the summer. Those highly sensitive to poison ivy should take precautions and attempt to perform the task before the sap is freely flowing in spring; botanically, smoketree is closely related to the malevolent *Toxicodendron pubescens* and *T. radicans*. In fact, it was once classified in the same genus as poison oak and poison ivy.

For vertical lines possessing the same rich pigment, several specimens of *Berberis thunbergii* 'Helmond Pillar', certainly too many, were planted early on. It remains a respectable if not somewhat pedestrian upright and narrow deciduous shrub but is prone to being pulled apart during winter snows; cinching the shrubs with twine helps in this matter. It also broadens with age (don't we all?)—thus, many have been removed as the garden has matured and choicer plants have gained an obligatory height.

The evergreen genus of *Pittosporum* gets good play as well, both on the bluff, where New Zealand species reign, and throughout the northern portion of the property, where Asian species dominate. *Pittosporum tenuifolium*, or *kohukohu* in the Maori tongue, is endemic to New Zealand and widespread on both islands. Rather plastic in its physical manifestation, the shrub or small tree is represented by no fewer than five cultivars on the bluff, all decidedly atypical of naturally occurring forms.

While its tiny dark purple flowers, hidden beneath the foliage, pulse an unexpectedly strong perfume after sunset, this species, used liberally across the bluff and terrace, is included for its form, foliage, and height—and I simply don't care what you think about that. It is interesting to note that numerous self-sown seedlings appear on a yearly basis that are obviously hybrids of the numerous cultivars I grow.

The daisy shrubs in the genus *Olearia* need special mention. The entire lot of them, Kiwis and Australians by nativity, are evergreen and enticingly distinct

ABOVE · *Cotinus coggygria* 'Royal Purple' plays well with *Miscanthus sinensis* 'Malepartus' in late autumn.

OPPOSITE · The color of *C. coggygria* 'Royal Purple' is most intense in autumn.

Vertical red lines of *Berberis thunbergii* 'Helmond Pillar' irregularly pierce the melee of ground-hugging plants near the upper fire pit on the terrace.

from one another. For fragrance, as already noted, I rely (a lot) on *Olearia* ×*oleifolia* 'Waikariensis' for its polite mounded habit, smothered in coconut-oil-scented flowers in July and gray-green foliage throughout the year.

The finely textured, golden-hued *Olearia virgata* is remarkable in toughness, while *O. ilicifolia* and *O. macrodonta* each provide an individual take on a tingly edged and tough presence with early summer clusters of white daisies. *Olearia* ×*haastii* and *O. phlogopappa* are similar to one another, the latter bearing somewhat larger leaves and blossoming later than other species in the genus, with nonspiny, glossy foliage and handsome white flowers in midsummer.

ABOVE · One species, two wildly different cultivars: the conical glistening silver-gray foliage of *Pittosporum tenuifolium* 'Tasman Ruffles' contrasts with dwarf mounds of *P. tenuifolium* 'County Park Dwarf' along the edge of the bluff.

ABOVE LEFT · *Pittosporum tenuifolium* 'County Park Dwarf' shows lime green new growth against its black winter foliage.

Olearia ×oleifolia 'Waikariensis', a daisy shrub from the South Island of New Zealand, is among the most valued shrubs that have settled in, offering a tidy evergreen habit along with summer fragrance and virtually no need for maintenance.

And finally, the twiggy tree daisy, *Olearia lineata* 'Dartonii', is remarkable as a durable, fast-growing doppelgänger of an olive tree, with narrow gray-green foliage and small fragrant white flowers in summer. It would easily reach thirty feet in height if we let it. We don't. The plant is cut hard in late winter to keep it to suitable proportions.

Olearia lineata
'Dartonii' nestles
up to the railing of
the deck outside
the guest quarters,
alongside the yellow
blossoms of the North
African *Adenocarpus
decorticans*.

The Circle

Robert and I were legally married in 2013, having waited until it was a federally recognized fundamental right rather than simply legal in our state. To commemorate our for-crying-out-loud-at-long-last-legal union, we commissioned a local iron artist, Ray Hammer, to forge a simple circle that Robert and I, working alone, hung from the branches of the bluffside madrona. The beast, twelve feet in diameter, was heavy and awkward to hang, a task that Robert and I accomplished together in a calm and trouble-free process that caused nary a mean word between the newly betrothed (who had already been living together for thirty years). Suspended on a free hinge, by complete serendipity the Circle generally stalls at an angle that best frames distant views of Bainbridge Island, including Bloedel Reserve, from various vantage points.

Windcliff-grown, open-pollinated agapanthus and our own selection of crocosmia, *Crocosmia pottsii* 'Butterbluff', commingle in a view corridor leading to the Circle.

Some Subshrubs for Sun

TRY SAYING THAT FIVE TIMES FAST after a couple glasses of summer chardonnay. I have been too taken by the performance of those that fall back without fully surrendering during the winter months to not give them the mention
they deserve.

Beginning in mid-April, clusters of porcelain blue, butterscotch-centered
flowers of *Solanum crispum* 'Glasnevin' are presented in large clusters amid
arching canes carrying glossy evergreen foliage. I first met this Chilean in the
garden of the late, enormously talented botanical illustrator Kevin Nicolay
(who also shared cuttings of it with me). On occasion, if left unstopped, it will
lean into one of the *Trachycarpus* specimens like James Dean slouching on a
wall while smoking a cigarette, and climb to commingle its blueness with the
tumble of golden blossoms of the palm, performing a memorable duet.

In some areas of the garden, *Fuchsia magellanica* in its raw state from wild
collections in Chile in 1998, 2005, and 2011 has created impenetrable thickets
of rounded shrubs rising to six feet. These shrubs have become the chosen
nesthold for legions of Anna's hummingbirds that have taken their maiden

Commonly known as the purple
potato vine, *Solanum crispum*
'Glasnevin' blossoms with *Euphorbia
characias*, another quasi-tolerated
self-sower in the garden.

flights in our garden. The fact that I couldn't care less if they have become overly rampant in the garden cannot be emphasized enough. Nearly twenty years on, I have not had any jump the fence.

From May through November, or perpetually should we have a mild winter, there is not just a steady drizzle of fuchsia flowers but a downright downpour. We have distributed two clones that arose with especially good floral attributes and compactness: 'Windcliff Flurry' and the more euphonious 'Windcliff Driveway'.

Romneya coulteri, the appositely named fried egg plant, does not sow itself about on our bluff, as fire is part and parcel of its procreational requirements in its native California and Baja California. This species failed to launch at Heronswood but has found purchase on the bluff at Windcliff, even becoming a bit thuggish through its rampant stoloniferous growth. Yet, calling our large colony a garden hoodlum would be akin to likening Audrey Hepburn to J. Edgar Hoover, a realization reached when reveling in its five-foot stems cloaked in blue-green foliage in full blossom on a sunny day in early July with a light breeze.

ABOVE · The nectar-rich flowers of *Fuchsia magellanica* are irresistible to our native hummingbirds, its pollinator of choice in its homeland of the southern Andes, while succulent berries captivate a winged throng of foragers.

OPPOSITE · Subshrub-like in mild winters, the inestimable California poppy, *Romneya coulteri*, floats its delicate flowers amid the sparklers of *Stipa gigantea* in early to mid July.

I encountered *Indigofera heterantha* while walking through Highgrove, the garden of HRH Prince Charles, with Robert and the late Rosemary Verey in the early 1990s. There was a large swath of it growing near the terrace, and Ms. Verey, being privileged to do such things in his garden, offered me some seed. The resulting plants have entertained me ever since with an endless progression of pink flowers in late summer, presented in short, upright racemes above finely fretted pinnate foliage. Propagules from the original collection with royal provenance have made their way onto the bluff, kindly reminding me of that memorable day years ago.

Likewise, I was introduced to *Indigofera pendula* in Roy Lancaster's classic *Travels in China* long before I encountered it growing in open pineland near Lijiang in Yunnan Province in 1996. With long, elegant floral chains, ultimately expanding to fifteen inches by summer's end, it often befuddles visitors to Heronswood and Windcliff alike who believe they are seeing a transmuted form of wisteria. It is best considered a freestanding multistemmed small tree and not cut back in spring as we do its brethren.

Little South Africa

THE OPULENT BOTANY OF SOUTH AFRICA has had a profound impact in gardens around the world and especially so in assembling a palette that works well and carries the seasons at Windcliff. *Agapanthus, Gladiolus, Kniphofia, Eucomis, Crocosmia, Watsonia, Dierama, Melianthus, Crinum, Amaryllis,* and *Phygelius* are a few of the familiar genera from this florally fat-cat region that have flourished here, some to a degree of discomfort, a few holding on for dear life.

Among the aristocrats of plants incorporated primarily for foliage effects is the giant honey flower, *Melianthus major,* a common denizen of the southwestern Cape, where it grows in parched, disturbed sites, often on roadside verges. Though somewhat raw in appearance in nature, it becomes a swan in the garden with a bit of coddling. The jagged-edged blue-green leaves, to fifteen inches in length, are carried on shrubby stems to five feet or slightly more in height. In early spring, tubular deep burgundy flowers, heavily scented of honey, are borne above the foliage. Because the flowers are produced on second-year growth, flowering will occur only if it is not cut to the ground by winter (or pruners). Unless I simply do not get to the task in time, we don't generally see the flowers, opting to cut the plants back hard before growth resumes in spring, regardless of how severe the preceding winter has been.

I learned of the charms of *Dierama* by way of the late Sue Buckles, a gentle yet exuberant Seattle gardener with British roots. She used wandflowers

Indigofera pendula blooms from late May until mid-autumn. The plants on our bluff are from the original collections I made in Yunnan Province in 1996.

ABOVE · We named this sensational ultrablue form of *Melianthus major* for Steve Antonow, the late gifted gardener from Seattle who shared it with us.

ABOVE RIGHT · My own collection of *Phygelius aequalis* from the Drakensberg Mountains in 2004 might have been discussed along with the subshrubs, as this plant remains upright and evergreen throughout the year. Though adored by hummingbirds, the plant's stoloniferous potency is equal to that of El Chapo's prison breaks.

brilliantly along steps in her garden, giving their arching canes access to the ungardened air above the concrete. Later, at Great Dixter, the home and garden of Christopher Lloyd in East Sussex, we together enjoyed afternoon tea on what is dubbed the Solar Terrace, where wandflowers arose and blossomed from every crack and cranny in the slate as well as the surrounding rock wall. These seedlings might have been removed by gardeners less tolerant of such exuberance than Christo. Sitting within a field of moving pendulous bells was nothing short of magic.

Attempting to create the same effect at Windcliff, granting them as much territory as they pleased for resowing, was a given by the time I began planting

the bluff. It was a plant I was long denied at Heronswood. Now that we have undeniably drier, warmer winters, they can be enjoyed in both gardens, but still, it is at Windcliff that they have stood up and sung. *Dierama adelphicum* is the first wandflower to blossom among the species and selections we have established, followed by the white form of *D. pulcherrimum* and the diminutive salmon-red-flowering *D. dracomontanum*, collected in the Drakensberg Mountains of South Africa in 2004. *Dierama pulcherrimum* in its many-hued color forms, as well as the distinctive *D. trichorhizum* with small lavender flowers, will follow. Working through the weave and tangle of stems in flower or seed makes for a season I look forward to each year.

Melianthus major 'Purple Haze', a compact selection made by legendary plantsman Roger Raiche, is less hardy than other clones we grow.

Dierama pulcherrimum
almost seems to be
deliberately working its
way home, self-sowing
amidst its compatriots
Agapanthus and *Elegia
capensis*.

ABOVE · *Dierama adelphicum* is the first wandflower to blossom on the bluff.

OPPOSITE · The sensory experience of walking through the weave and tangle of *Dierama pulcherrimum* in flower on the bluff is reason enough to grow it here.

Though few other summer perennials add such a saucy and torrid display as *Crocosmia* in the dog days of summer, when tubular flowers in a spectrum of spicy colors erupt from clumps of pleated green or tastefully bronzed irislike foliage, I have a very sincere "meh" moment with most I now encounter. At one time, an entire area of the garden was devoted to a pasture of this genus, with many of the selections of our own making while we operated Heronswood Nursery. The best have been retained. The worst we will never be rid of.

Crocosmias are produced from corms not unlike those of a very small gladiolus, from which rhizomes spread outward to form substantial colonies over time—and in some cases, we are talking Manhattan substantial. Long Island substantial. California substantial. It is the length of the rhizome of each species or hybrid that determines the density of the plants, separating the Libras from the Virgos. The Libras of the clan, with rhizomes the length of a gorilla's arm, have soured me on the group as a whole. I have spent much too much time attempting to rid myself of *Crocosmia* 'Culzean Peach' (such a lovely name, he thought), all the while cognizant of the fact that I did this to myself, to ever consider planting another.

ABOVE · *Crocosmia* 'Coleton Fishacre' grows with scarlet *Lobelia tupa* from Chile at the base of the prayer flags.

LEFT · The dieramas are pure magic, blooming in summer and then carrying their globular seed heads on willowy moving stems into autumn, amidst *Phygelius aequalis* 'Moonrake'. Both hail from South Africa.

The "pokers" of South Africa, however, never cease to entertain. The show goes on from the later days of winter, when *Kniphofia northiae* present unlikely large orange orbs atop broad agave-like rosettes of foliage, until early October, when the flowers of *K. drepanophylla* appear, so cool within their clumps of tall, sturdy, thin grasslike foliage, so classy.

Agapanthus

A MADNESS FOR and a beguilement with the genus *Agapanthus* exists on the bluff. Agape. Astonished. And that I have in some insignificant way improved upon the genus through a passive selection process is a myth, *ben trovato*, of my own making.

More than three decades ago, I was offered a division of a supposedly tender agapanthus from an elderly but passionate gardener who had coddled it in a container for many years. She had her division of this plant, she told me, from a friend's bluffside garden in Indianola. My division of this plant, which I called *Agapanthus africanus*, ultimately overfilled a large container in the garden at Heronswood, offering its spherules of blue flowers on erect stems to three feet, held above strappy evergreen foliage in mid to late summer. Ironically, when we moved that container to Windcliff, we were actually bringing that division back to its very origin.

Throughout our new garden, beefy clumps of agapanthus from which this division had first been offered were thriving comfortably as durable and drought-resistant plants. Witnessing how well this plant fared in the full sun and sandy soil of our new garden was pivotal in the love affair that commenced.

That very first agapanthus that I grew as *Agapanthus africanus* is in fact correctly known as *Agapanthus praecox*. This is a common species in cultivation, one that can be seen rather vulgarly employed in institutional plantings throughout much of California. The species and hybrids with a great deal of its blood are not generally hardy for us in the Pacific Northwest.

The gravelly bluff is cordial to *Agapanthus* as a whole, and a passive breeding and selection process is into its second decade in the garden, with seedlings blossoming in only a year from seed and evaluation of the two-hundred-plus seedlings planted each year commencing in only two years. Our selection program has been directed entirely toward those that fully lose their leaves in winter; those tending toward evergreenness will not tolerate temperatures below 20 degrees F, while the fully deciduous forms are surprisingly hardy.

Agapanthus campanulatus is a deciduous species, and one I consider to be the hardiest of the genus and the earliest to blossom. It is variable in color,

Honeybees and bumblebees, swallowtail butterflies, and Anna's and rufous hummingbirds do the work of transferring agapanthus pollen in my passive selection program

The slow, rolling deto-
nation of *Agapanthus*
begins just as the awns
of *Stipa gigantea* ripen
to their signature gilded
glitter.

from dark blue to pure white; however, those I observed in the wild at high elevations in the Drakensberg Mountains of South Africa were of a medium blue, blossoming on stems to two and a half feet tall. This was a good starting point for us.

During an earlier trip to South Africa, I fell madly for *Agapanthus inapterus*, one of the most distinctive of agapanthus species. Stems rising to five feet are capped by a descending floral progression in deep blue-violet tones. *Agapanthus inapterus* subsp. *pendulus* 'Graskop' is a superb selection with distinctive pendulous flowers of midnight blue opening from black buds atop sturdy stems to two and a half feet tall. "Astonishing" is an apt descriptor.

The best seed parents thus far have been *Agapanthus* 'Quink Drops'—a selection made by superb plantsman and friend Graham Gough of the United Kingdom—and *A.* 'Queen Mum', despite the fact that the latter is not hardy for us. The former has given us the lion's share of our best Windcliff selections.

A generous planting of agapanthus displays variations of color and form from a single seed parent, 'Queen Mum'.

Agapanthus 'Vivian Clara' is named for my mother, who was neither present nor disorderly during the evening many of our plants were baptized with names during our wedding celebration in 2013.

During our wedding celebrations in 2013, which lasted longer than the average Ramadan, special guests were allowed to pick out their favorite plant among the countless seedlings in full blossom on our bluff, a market research scheme involving several bottles of wine and a congregation of female fighters and stalwarts who were provided with labels with their names to adhere to their favorite plants. The resulting selections from that evening were named after each jury member and have become part of the Formidable Women of Windcliff Series.

The satisfaction of working within this genus comes after the selection process, when the anointed are divided and planted in larger clonal groups, providing more punch. It is not just the color or deepness of hue nor the size of flower or height of stem that we evaluate. Timing of flowering also becomes part of the consideration process in our attempt to extend their theatrical season into late September and early October. Many of our agapanthus selections will never become part of a greater marketing plan because their tall stems make them difficult to distribute. However, it is precisely their stature that I am attracted to, especially when those of differing heights are planted cheek by jowl.

Given that we are selecting for deciduous members of *Agapanthus*, the garden space reserved for the plants is entirely vacated after the first hard frosts. Pairing the plants with elements that carry the garden through the off months is important. Until it is necessary to cut them down, we leave the flowering stems unmolested to provide migrating and resident birds a bit of nourishment and a place to perch above ground level.

Attempting to divide any agapanthus will provide notice to the observant gardener that these plants are serious about survival. The root systems are nearly impenetrable mats of chunky white water-retentive roots, indicative of the drought tolerance of the genus as a whole. Regular division does not seem to be remotely imperative, though those wishing to do it will find it an honest workout. One caveat: allow plenty of room when planting among the impregnable tatami of agapanthus roots for initial establishment of companion plants.

Whether this exceptional genus of African plants is planted en masse, positioned singularly in a mixed border, or maintained in containers, few perennials can equal the lasting effects of its color and form. Even in climates too cold to cultivate any agapanthus directly in the garden, the genus as a whole does remarkably well in containers; fertilize your plants amply in late summer with formulations meant to promote flowering.

Grasses

SEDGES HAVE EDGES, rushes are round, grasses, my lasses, are hollow, I've found. I guess I finally got it, while under the influence of a glass of sauvignon blanc on the northeastern corner of the North Island of New Zealand. For the record, I am not really a sauvignon blanc sort of guy, but asking for an oaky chardonnay in that region is akin to ordering a peaty scotch in Dublin. But I digress. It was 2001; I was in New Zealand to speak at a conference and had the pleasure of listening to the opening act, British garden designer Dan Pearson, and the misfortune of having to follow him on the dais. His gardens and the plants he employs were described in a humble, quiet poetry that I will never forget. He spoke of grasses and their diaphanous qualities. They hold the light and communicate the movement of air—or the lack of it, he said.

We owned Windcliff, and I was ready at last to accept his observations as truth. I returned home a convert.

Before I go any farther, I should acknowledge there were others whom I considered friends at the time—and still do—who preached the same gospel. Rick Darke, John Greenlee, and Piet Oudolf, all of whom I respected for their knowledge of and passion for grasses, had failed to persuade this philistine. Wolfgang Oehme and James van Sweden, too, employed grasses in large installations. I remained nonplussed. I gardened at Heronswood.

Grasses are principally about movement and then about capturing light while letting some photons pass through them. The images by Claire Takacs in this book effectively—sensationally—capture the secondary attribute. Yet my

RIGHT · Spring anticipation is in full bore as the grasses emerge in a shade of green that only gardeners can appreciate.

OPPOSITE TOP · Early in the season, *Scilla peruviana* emerges among the sturdy roots of agapanthus and foretells the deep colors that will come later in the season.

OPPOSITE BOTTOM · Particularly good agapanthus seedlings from the Windcliff selection program, now named, create a river of blue running across the bluff in early August.

Stipa gigantea is allowed to self-sow within reason and provides a remarkable showing in movement and capture of light while in blossom.

underlying reason for their use cannot be approximated by a still image. It is the dance, the nod, and the play of grass foliage and flowers that fully animates the garden at Windcliff.

Exploiting their strengths effectually presented me with a precipitous learning curve, including consideration of siting and spacing as well as which species to employ and, more important, which ones to shun entirely.

Like all good plants that catch the fancy of a passionate gardener, grasses can be overdone. I was drawn off course by believing the breadth of sky and the stretch of horizon demanded sweeps of everything I planted, more so the grasses that would be used as the substrate of plantings on the bluff. I was quite wrong.

I initially planted *Cortaderia* and *Molinia* species in groups of seven, nine, and fifteen, while allowing *Stipa tenuissima* (syn. *Nassella tenuissima*) to self-sow to the degree it wished, editing only in the pathways. Within just three years, I was tackling a major correction of my mistakes. Anyone who has grown pampas grass for three years understands that removing a mature specimen is not a matter of hitting Control-Delete. It is a full day's effort; small charges of C-4 are not entirely off the table.

I had managed to create barriers of foliage and flower that negated any grace, dance, or accentuation inherently possessed by the grasses. I could neither look through them nor around them.

There were some especially terrible choices. I have included, and then eradicated, thrice the number of grass species that I currently cultivate on the bluff. *Chionochloa rubra* from New Zealand is everbrown, conjuring a forgettable and lengthy death scene at the zenith of its beauty. *Anemanthele lessoniana* (syn. *Stipa arundinacea*) is gorgeous. Buy one and every garden in your county will enjoy its charms within a year. The same might be true for *Stipa tenuissima*. I was less stern with its self-sowing proclivities than I should have been; I loved its fine, silken qualities of foliage and flower as it bleached in late summer and moved with the slightest breath of air. It was not until its sharpened awns sent two of our dogs to the vet to have them removed from their throats that I realized its sadistic qualities. This grass is no longer welcome in the garden, but it will be many years before it is fully eradicated.

The previously mentioned pampas grass, *Cortaderia selloana*, especially its dwarf form 'Compacta', is contemptible, bringing forth in flower a regrettable image of Humpty Dumpty in RuPaul regalia.

However, there are some grasses I would not be without, planted singularly and interrupted with differing textures and heights. The autumn moorgrass, *Molinia caerulea*, and many of its selections are outstanding. *Molina caerulea* 'Heidebraut' is a compact affair to fifteen inches high, while 'Strahlenquelle' is

midheight, to two and a half feet in full blossom. *Molinia caerulea* subsp. *arundinacea* 'Skyracer' is aptly named, adding hazy plumes to six feet or more from tidy two-foot mounds of foliage. These are clumping, long-lived plants that only rarely self-sow.

Autumn switch grass, *Panicum virgatum*, is indispensable. *Panicum virgatum* 'Dallas Blues' has a superlative blue-green cast to its leaves, and it flowers in airy panicles above four-foot columns of foliage in September. Numerous red-foliaged forms, such as 'Shenandoah', continue to become available, but I have not found their vigor to be adequate, perhaps due to where I have them

ABOVE · As the skies darken and temperatures plummet in mid-November, the garden solidifies in growth and intensifies in color. Especially good all the way through to midwinter are the *Panicum* species.

ABOVE LEFT · Numerous forms of *Molinia caerulea* with differing heights are highly valued minions of the bluff.

planted, nor their fall color to be consistent. Hands-down best is 'Northwind', with erect, nonflopping columns of dark green foliage providing movement in summer while the structure remains intact long into winter after the foliage has transitioned to delicious butterscotch tones. In full disclosure, while I was writing this very section on grasses, we received welcome and significant but unusual September rain, resulting in the most sincere form of flopping of my nonflopping specimens of 'Northwind'.

Of *Miscanthus*, I am somewhat embarrassed by the inclusion of *M. sinensis* 'Cabaret'. Its broad white-striped foliage does not fit the scheme, and I have too much of it, planted much too close to one another. The more elegant *M. sinensis* 'Malepartus' is planted individually, erupting from an expanse of *Agapanthus*, adding both contrasting foliage texture and flower differential that makes it all work.

For kinetics alone, not to mention weeks upon weeks of effective blossom, I remain committed to *Austroderia richardii* (syn. *Cortaderia fulvida*). What has

Columnar *Panicum virgatum* 'Northwind' is the hands-down best switch grass.

Austroderia richardii,
from New Zealand,
erupts in a whiter shade
of pale in June and
continues with a bob
and a dance throughout
autumn.

been passed about in cultivation under this name may not be valid. None the matter—it is the maestro of the entire orchestrated garden when in blossom. Its golden dusters nod gently atop eight-foot stems, brightening to platinum as the season progresses. Birds landing on the flowering stems and bobbing, seemingly for pure entertainment, add to the joy. I play somewhat with fire as I find the occasional self-sown seedling.

But genuine bliss comes from the earliest of them all. *Stipa gigantea* is a Eurasian steppe species forming tidy clumping rosettes of green foliage to one foot, from which arises a surprisingly out-of-proportion gilded sparkle of flowers in early June that remains effective well into August. This grass has politely self-sown here and there, with each seedling producing varying flowering heights, from three to seven feet. The flowers glitter bomb when the sun catches them in the right position and the wind is calm, while curtsying politely or wildly whirling when the winds arise.

On cool, humid, still days in early March, I take a torch to my grasses, avoiding adjacent shrubs and trees as much as my pyromania will allow me. The chore is over in only an hour. Occasionally, quite by accident, I set one of my windmill palms on fire, which appears at that moment rather biblical. They are never seriously damaged. The grasses themselves tell me when it is

THIS PAGE · In mid-June, silky, diaphanous heads of *Stipa gigantea* arise from tidy evergreen mounds of foliage, later unfastening to a sparkle of gold, effective throughout the summer into autumn.

OPPOSITE · *Rhodocoma capensis* provides a swirling frame for *Yucca rostrata*, with *Taxus baccata* 'Aureovariegata' in the foreground.

time they depart the scene, as the foliage begins to shatter and blow about the garden, escalating the errand of spring cleanup. Many of the winter-dormant grasses, however, are left alone until then, providing an arresting color of amber, the ever-important movement, and roosting habitat as well as food for resident and migrating birds while slowly decomposing, enriching the edaphic environment.

Give It a Restio

CONSIDER A CLUMPING CREATURE with feathery shags of green foliage on stems rising to six feet. In early spring, the new stems gather up like spears of hallucinating bamboo, sheathed in a Moody Blues arrangement of pinks, crimsons, greens, grays, and indigoes. In a likeness to fine ceramic, it is a tasteful yet daring combination of colors that at once makes you wish to grow it, cut it, and eat it, though the latter is not among the alternatives, to the best of my knowledge. Meet *Rhodocoma capensis*.

Rhodocoma is one of numerous genera found within a family of grass allies, the family Restionaceae. But for a couple of wayward species native to New

Zealand and Australia, the entire family is found in South Africa, in particular the fynbos of the southwestern Cape.

My pride and joy remains *Cannomois virgata*, the most graceful and imposing of the South African restios. All others pale in comparison to its tall, gracefully arching stems laden with pendulous, plumy foliage. I sited it in a drier location closer to the house for protection, as it has proven to be tender. Tucked into a protected planting pocket on the terrace, it softens the mean-spiritedness of *Agave salmiana* while offering an agile dance of foliage in the winds of winter. This was my holy grail of the entire tribe, and my specimen still stirs a sinful pride; I have it and you probably don't and never will.

Elegia capensis has also found its way into our garden, and its habit adds to the effect of spring growth with burgundy and white shieldlike bracts held along stems from which whorls of spidery green foliage unfurl. It has succeeded well on the bluff and elicits a familiar refrain from virtually everyone meeting it for the first time: "Too bad about the horsetail." It is indeed a doppelgänger of that treacherous weed, though taller and entirely clumping by nature. I find seeing its clean, feathery, acidic green new growth in spring akin to taking a shower with peppermint soap after a long, hot day in the garden. Lit by a low-angled sun, it creates an arousing display as the agapanthus comes into bloom nearby.

I've not succeeded as well with *Chondropetalum tectorum*, a tall, nearly leafless, rushlike plant with growth to six feet; each stem is interrupted by regularly spaced sheaths of suede-leather brown. When well grown, it becomes a five-by-five-foot bundle of fiber optics; poorly grown, it simply

ABOVE · *Elegia capensis* shows remarkably colorful new growth in spring

TOP ROW · *Rhodocoma capensis* is dioecious, with male (shown here) and female flowers on different plants, though little else but the flowers is discernibly different between the sexes. The new growth in spring is decidedly erect and develops its weighty shag of green as the season progresses.

Cannomois virgata was my holy grail of the entire tribe of restios and is sited near the mean-spirited *Agave salmiana* on the terrace.

dies. I am attempting it again as a container plant, in both a Lilliputian form shared with me by Ed Bowen of Rhode Island and as one of more natural proportions.

The family is chock full, with many more genera and species than are implied in this short treatise on their worthiness. Though I continue to trial as many as I can when afforded the opportunity, the majority are better adapted to true Mediterranean climates and not proven winners in our own.

The best source of restio seed is Silverhill Seeds in Cape Town, South Africa. The enterprise is still in business after the proprietors, Rod and Rachel Saunders, friends with whom I spent time in the field in 2003 and 2004, were senselessly and tragically kidnapped and murdered while gathering seed in the Eastern Cape in 2017. Their generous spirit and dedication to examining and sharing the floral richness of their country is quite alive in a prayer flag raised in their memory on our bluff.

The Council Ring

The council ring is the heart of the garden.

OPPOSITE · Jeffrey Bale's work outside of the council ring evokes our beach at low tide with ripples of sand, exposed starfish, and sand dollars.

The council ring, or in Michigan-speak our fire pit, was built as the heart of the garden while offering guidance on the ultimate siting of the house as well as the detailing of the interiors, loosely described as heavily-marine-invertebrate-influenced craftsman-Asian style. Jeffrey Bale, now considered the maestro of mosaic, began construction in 2002, proceeding with a design we collaboratively agreed upon that would cele-brate the clever giant Pacific octopus, the world's largest, which calls home the waters directly beyond our bluff.

We watched with fascination as Jeffrey composed its portrayal over the course of six weeks from rocks and pebbles he hand selected from our beach below and sorted for color. A few

meaningful rocks from my youth—fossilized coral known as Petoskey stones, gathered from the shores of Lake Michigan near my mom's home-town of Arcadia—are assimilated randomly into the design.

Four of the tentacles that wrap the walls indicate the cardinal points, while two of the remaining four point to the summer solstice sunrise and the longest day's sunset, respec-tively. A tranquil-faced sun, carved in stone by Marcia Donahue, indicates due south, while the entrance to the ring itself, at Jeffrey's insistence and based on edicts of Eastern philosophy, is due east. One must now be abraded by the needle-sharp foliage of *Berberis* (*Mahonia*) *pinnata* 'Ken Hartman' to enter the ring's inner

sanctum in the accepted manner, another edict.

The council ring, as we had hoped, has become the heart of the garden and a place where fires and picnics have brought together on nights too numerous to recall a legion of friends from across the country and the world. It is the only part of the severe bluff edge that allows a satiating drink of the entirety of the view Windcliff now possesses. With or without a fire, the installation contains enough memories already embedded in its stones to keep us quite warm for years to come.

Marcia Donahue's peaceful sun indicates due south.

The House and Terrace

The house was designed to nestle close to the earth and not impose upon the landscape. The orientation reflects the curvature of the bluff edge, taking advantage of distinct views from each quarter.

Ultimately, the paths of our independent studies—Robert's house and my garden—had to cross. The decisions I initially made in the garden set the course for adjusting, just to the tiniest degree, the design of the house, while the house itself—with a few selfless compromises on my part—became a celebration of the garden.

THE HOUSE AND TERRACE

The House

PEG'S AND MARY'S EXISTING HOME at Windcliff was designed by Robert Shields of the Seattle firm Tucker, Shields and Terry. A wall of glass on the southern side captured one of the most dramatic views of Puget Sound we had ever seen, but without operable windows it also gathered an uncomfortable degree of heat. The smaller interior spaces on the north side of the house were as unnaturally dark as their southerly counterparts were overly warm.

Balancing architectural significance against the changes we would ultimately proceed with in extensive remodeling seemed to require sensitivity. And retaining the footprint of the existing house would aid us in clearing the hoops and hurdles that getting permits for new construction on the waterfront would have presented.

After spending weekends in the house for nearly three years cogitating on means to mitigate its shortcomings, we ultimately decided to simply repurpose the interior's clear cedar paneling and a redesigned kitchen into an independent basement apartment, and reconfigure the existing structure, while adding on two wings. Robert, the in-house architect, sharpened his pencils during those weekends when I was planting perimeter screening and reducing the inherited massive expanse of mown turf. Our two very disparate projects had in their futures an intersection and melding, but those first broad strokes were not fully coordinated with one another.

Ask any architect their idea of the ultimate nightmare client, and most would finger their spouse. Robert was as passionate about designing and building this home within our budget as I was about creating a garden in

The house and property in June 2000, soon after we purchased it, provided us with enormous potentials as well as serious challenges. The south-facing wall of glass proffered spectacular views but resulted in a stifling interior during the summer months.

such a setting as Windcliff. The difficulty lay in my inability to understand what came naturally to him—converting a two-dimensional drawing into a three-dimensional object.

To his credit, Robert did not critique my choice of plants or planting design—Precisely how might such brilliance be criticized?—and so, somewhat radically, I left the house to his talents. I had only three requests. ("Per day," he might add.)

1. The house at Heronswood, a very small and simple but ultimately warm and accommodating 1970s rambler, served more as a rarely vacant hotel with good fare for visiting horticulturists than as our home. The three small bedrooms were cheek by jowl on the eastern end of the house. At Windcliff, I insisted that, using the cosmic distance ladder, if our bedroom was the Sun of our solar system, I wanted guests sequestered on one of the moons of Neptune.

2. In the autumn of 2000, just months after purchasing our property and years before we began construction, I spent time botanizing in northeast Turkey, where more often than not we stayed with local farmers in small villages. Our communal quarters would be on the top floor with a solid roof above but fully open sides; we slept on fine carpets that lined the floors. Home again, I suggested that one of our rooms be a variation on this theme with walls of glass that would open to invite the outside in.

3. In 1999, just before the millennial celebrations, we spent Christmas with Christopher Lloyd and Fergus Garrett at Great Dixter, where we had been guests many times before. Holiday celebrations at Dixter were centered in the Great Hall, one of two fifteenth-century banquet halls brought together by Lutyens in 1910 under the direction of Christo's parents. During that week of tremendous gales, we warmed ourselves with fire and scotch near the immense hearth and feasted with friends under ancient oak beams festooned with garlands. Memories of that trip and the Great Hall influenced a significant part of our new home. I wanted a fireplace large enough to roast an entire cow.

Robert's design, with virtually imperceptible suggestions on my part, resulted in three pavilions joined by glass-enclosed connectors. The kitchen, living room, and guest quarters would occupy the footprint of the existing house. To the far west he designed a new master bedroom suite, and between

The house at Windcliff
erodes from view during
high summer when
dieramas and grasses
approach the zenith of
their growth cycles.

them, perpendicular to these structures, a large hall and library pavilion. While the house was deliberately designed to not impose itself on the landscape, its siting was based less on potential views from the interior and more on communication with the views framed by existing trees along with a sense of privacy from adjoining properties.

A Turkish-inspired open-air dining room in the connector between the kitchen and the large hall and a similar connector containing our offices between the hall and the master suite tether the three pavilions together. These two bridges, the dining room and offices, are significantly narrower than the adjoining construction, creating alcoves on both the north and south sides.

The waterside alcoves became a part of the sun-drenched terrace and deck wrapping the south side of the house. The shaded, protected alcoves on the north side provide sheltered growing conditions for delicate plants resentful of blasting wind and sun, and an intimate space to display art.

The dining alcove on the north side of the house is particularly handsome in texture during the growing season, with a distinguished assemblage of shade-loving plants from my collections, including *Fatsia polycarpa* collected in Taiwan in 1999. Another rarity, also in the family Araliaceae, is *Merrilopanax alpinus*, a small, deciduous, large-leaved tree from the Sikkimese Himalaya. Beneath these plantings, the ground is carpeted with a mosaic of *Arachniodes standishii* (Korea, 1997), *Woodwardia unigemmata* (Taiwan, 1999), *Begonia pedatifida* (China, 1996), *Begonia palmata* (Myanmar, 2013), and *Ruscus colchicus* (Turkey, 2000).

The office alcove boasts a rambunctious grove of "Bambusa maritima," a play in clay heavily salted with marine associations—including octopus tentacles, sand dollars, and sea urchins—by renowned sculptor, ceramicist, and textile artist Marcia Donahue, whose infatuating work in clay and stone can be found throughout the house and garden. Spears of new evergreen growth to six feet on *Disporum longistylum* 'Green Giant' (collected in Sichuan in 1996) appear uncannily similar to Donahue's playful work.

This protective niche disports the original *Schefflera taiwaniana* clone from Taiwan that I introduced to cultivation in 1999. Though I have made subsequent seed collections of this species, and numerous clones from my

ABOVE · *Disporum longistylum*, in both foliage and spears of new growth, associates well with Marcia Donahue's installation.

TOP · The office alcove is home to "Bambusa maritima" by Marcia Donahue and the original *Schefflera taiwaniana* (Taiwan, 1999).

OPPOSITE · The northern dining alcove features Mark Bulwinkle's fanciful rusted metal bamboo and an antique stone basin, a house-warming gift from Robert's parents upon our purchasing Heronswood. *Fatsia polycarpa* dominates with broad, palmate foliage.

work and others make the circuit in commerce, it is satisfying to retain the mother of so many plants, which alerted gardeners to both the hardiness and charms of this genus.

Accentuating the marine-invertebrate theme, herbaceous components include many good plants that span the seasons and represent the outcome of numerous trips abroad. Two mayapples provide broad, highly textural leaves with kelp-like qualities: *Podophyllum delavayi* (Sichuan, 1996) possesses blotches and bloats of black-purple on satin green, while the foliage of *P. pleianthum* (Taiwan, 1999) is hexagonal and glossy green with a decidedly tropical punch.

A particularly good and rarely found form of the Hart's tongue fern, *Asplenium scolopendrium* 'Dixter', given to me by Christopher Lloyd in the mid-1990s, thrives along with *Disporopsis arisanensis* (Taiwan, 1999) and *Paris vietnamensis* (Vietnam, 1999), creating a rich fabric at the base of Marcia's bamboo. Perhaps the most acceptable of the Jack-in-the-pulpits, *Arisaema taiwanensis* (Taiwan, 1999), reseeds here liberally.

Both alcoves are meant to be dioramas viewed entirely from inside the house. In particular, the dining alcove cannot be fully appreciated from its outdoor vantage. The upside of this approach is that in high season, for those seated at the dining table, an arid Mediterranean hummingbird-infested garden gushes in from the south, while a cool, verdant forest floor from an Asian mountainside demands attention from the north. The downside . . . yes, there are always downsides. Planting, pruning, weeding, and even watering must often be performed by accessing the garden through the dining room. The resulting mare's nest often produces very disquieting evenings in our household.

Located at each end of the house, bathtub extensions surrounded by glass encourage the rare hot soaks that we imagined would become common after building such luxuries. In the master wing, on the infrequent occasions when I actually do take a long soak, I can gaze upon the tangerine-colored flowers of witch hazel, *Hamamelis ×intermedia* 'Aphrodite', in winter, while in early spring the pendulous, bisexual, richly colored plum racemes of *Akebia trifoliata* var. *australis*, which I grew from seed collected in northeastern Sichuan in 2003, is keenly backlit by the late afternoon sun. The vine thrives in the ridiculously bad unamended subsoil left behind from excavating the foundation of the house. An outdoor shower, used consistently after a day's gardening with a stone mosaic floor by Jeffrey Bale massaging one's feet, directs water to the afore-mentioned *Hamamelis*.

A wall of differing clones of *Daphne bholua*, in my mind the most beguilingly scented of all shrubs that I cultivate, envelops the bathtub of the guest wing.

THIS PAGE · Variation in foliage is shown between different clones of *Podophyllum delavayi*.

OPPOSITE · *Arisaema taiwanensis* thrives in the shelter and shade of the office alcove.

Two of the specimens, collected from higher elevations in northeastern Nepal in 2002, frequently drop their leaves in the winter—sorry about that privacy thing—while the primary screen of plants grown from seed from lower elevations in Sichuan Province, collected in 2006, remains evergreen. It is intriguing, to say the least, to witness the variations among individuals of this species that is widely distributed throughout Asia.

On warm(er) winter days, with doors open at both ends of the house, we enjoy a rich concoction of scents of daphne from one direction and witch hazel from the other, colliding like a happy accident between the two wings.

Akebia trifolia var. *australis* sports pendulous racemes in early spring.

Vines, Arbors, and Entrances

AS WE DESIGNED THE HOUSE, arbors dominated the major portals, north, south, east, and west. It would be on these structures that I would grow plants naturally suited to drape and cloak and, in the process, meld their support into a oneness of green. Though I have already mentioned the akebia that conceals the bathing area of the master bedroom, I will proceed to blather on about vines in general before I reveal which ones made the ultimate cut for adhering and entwining the house to the garden.

Total transparency: I love vines. In a gentle weave, or sometimes a more vigorous strangle, vining or climbing plants, unlike any other garden constituent, can amend their position in the landscape while seeking out the very best environment for their survival and—for us—their appearance. Their unpredictable and adventuresome behavior offers both serendipity and inspiration.

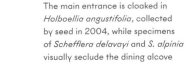

The main entrance is cloaked in *Holboellia angustifolia*, collected by seed in 2004, while specimens of *Schefflera delavayi* and *S. alpinia* visually seclude the dining alcove

Observation of countless species of vining plants in their native haunts, from Japan to Chile, Tasmania to Nepal, has writ large on my psyche this indisputable fact: vines did not co-evolve with arbors. Though the trellis, wall, or pergola may indeed be a superior choice for displaying twining plants, if the garden offers a framework of trees and shrubs, a natural down-market choice on which to support a vine already exists.

Taking advantage of this strategy serves the gardener in numerous ways. A bold-foliaged vine allowed to explore the framework of a more finely textured tree or shrub, or the converse, provides the textural contrast so paramount to any satisfying garden composition. A midsummer- or autumn-flowering vine clambering through a spring-blossoming tree or shrub lengthens the season of interest while taking full advantage of the often-neglected upper stratosphere of our landscapes. Further still, most climbers prove quick to establish, furnishing a patina to the garden that might otherwise take countless more growing seasons to achieve. Vines may be clever, but it is ultimately the cagey gardener who takes advantage of their strengths.

Why not take yet another cue from nature and combine two or more species of vines? Picture an early-blossoming clematis sharing an intimate moment with a late-blossoming clematis, both hopelessly entwined with an evergreen, midsummer-blossoming, fragrant honeysuckle. The mass becomes one as it sparkles in different seasons. We have to get over this rather bizarre notion that plants in our gardens must be segregated from one another. Often in nature I have seen an entanglement of different vines sharing the same vertical support. Insisting that vines are happier and comelier when planted alone is like inviting an intoxicatingly interesting list of guests to a dinner party and not allowing them to talk to one another.

Though I have set the stage to think of vines as solely vertical players in the garden, by nature they seek out their desired scaffolding by first growing horizontally in all directions. Before assuming that a vine must be grown vertically, consider first the remarkable cache of normally vining plant species that will make exceptional and unanticipated ground covers. The climbing hydrangea, *Hydrangea anomala*, though superlative when used as a self-clinging deciduous vine in shaded situations, becomes equally utilitarian when denied a vertical lift. Covering the ground along our drive we have a sizeable—okay, it has become much too large—plant of this species from seed collected on Ulleung Island, South Korea, in 1983. When in full blossom, it is remarkable.

Likewise, any clematis planted as a sprawling herbaceous perennial will delight with unexpected and serendipitous combinations; I am particularly fond of the genus when it chooses its own scaffolding on which to grow. How extraordinary it was to discover *Clematis chrysocoma*, a sensational

I have used *Hydrangea anomala* var. *petiolaris* as a ground-hugging vine. However, its propensity to climb is readily shown as it lifts into the support of *Clethra barbinervis*. Both were collected on the same trip to South Korea in 1993.

semi-scrambler I had collected in Yunnan Province in 2000, blossoming in perfect sync with *Olearia ilicifolia*, the so-called daisy shrub, the latter with clusters of delicate white composites. This had not been my intent.

Tropaeolum speciosum, a hardy vining nasturtium from Chile, is more sinned against than sinner. The vine was inadvertently transplanted to Windcliff, arriving as a stowaway in the roots of a shrub or tree brought from Heronswood. It is easy to reduce when it becomes too much of a good thing, though when it is in bloom with saucy red flowers coveted by hummingbirds, or in fruit with berries like sapphires held within a crimson purse, nimiety never seems a problem demanding an immediate solution.

And then there is the magic and mystery of the flowers of *Aristolochia* or Dutchman's pipe. Four species (*A. californica*, *A. griffithii*, *A. manshuriensis*, and *A. kaempferi*) have been turned loose on unsuspecting shrubs and trees in the garden at Windcliff. I also keep the latter contained in a pot near the front door to show visitors its fantastical means of procreation.

In April and May, *Aristolochia kaempferi* produces curiously beautiful, inflated "pipes" held pendulant from its leaf axils, providing ultimate viewing enjoyment when backlit by morning or evening light. Subtle odors from these curious flowers mimic the ideal brood cavity for midges and other flying insects, generally but not always particular to the species of *Aristolochia*. The flies, however, quickly find themselves held hostage in a one-way passage, while the flower hopes at least one of the unwilling guests has not arrived empty-handed but will deliver a tidbit of pollen to the inner works. Twenty-four hours later, or after fertilization is complete (it never pays to arrive early), the entire party is dusted with pollen and unceremoniously liberated. A botanical rendering of "Hotel California," it is one of the infinite mysteries sequestered in our gardens. The melodrama and intricate beauty of such plants is often what brings the next generation of gardeners into our fold.

So, at last, the big reveal—the divulging you have been restlessly waiting for. What vines made the grade for the stout arbors surrounding our entrances? In a word, the house was Lardizabalated. Being the extremely stable genius with unmatched wisdom that I am, I give you a word that has probably never been used before. It refers to my love of those members of the Lardizabalaceae, a family composed of mostly evergreen vines from Asia and South America. At the entrance, in addition to the aforementioned akebia, in the same family, is *Holboellia angustifolia*, whose large purple-rinded fruit I collected in Yunnan Province in 1996. Its flowers—not particularly large or showy—pack a powerful redolence, brought inside with each opening of the door in March and early April. On the southern side of the house I have used another species, *Holboellia latifolia*, with very pretty, faintly cinnamon-scented purple flowers and heavily

Clematis chrysocoma, collected in Yunnan in 2000, and *Olearia ilicifolia* weave through each other and blossom in concert in early June.

THIS PAGE · *Tropaeolum speciosum* ingratiates itself when in flower and fruit.

veined foliage that emerges in spring with burnished tones. I collected its fruit on a trek to the remote northeast of Nepal near a tiny settlement called Ritak. I was called into the house of a resident that day by his family and asked if I could help him as he lay dying on his bed; I had nothing in my bags to provide.

To the east, climbing through the railing of the deck is *Holboellia brachyandra*, whose fruit I shared with my guides and porters in a mountain hut on Fan Si Pan in Vietnam after a day of hard hiking. The flowers are large and white and held on pedicels of red amidst handsome trifoliate leaves never blemished by even the harshest temperatures our climate tosses at it. The seductive foliage

Aristolochia kaempferia shows off its mesmerizing floral design.

THIS PAGE · Fragrant blossoms of *Holboellia angustifolia* are followed by showy, edible fruits in fall.

of *Holboellia yaoshanensis*, collected in Vietnam in 1999, was good enough reason to grow it even without flower, although flowering did happen in spring 2019. All *Holboellia* are beautiful vines in flower and in fruit, but mostly they remain corridors of memories and moments that have shaped who I am as a person and as a gardener.

Another member of the family growing at Windcliff is worth mentioning. *Boquila trifoliolata*—from Chile, where I collected its seed with Dave Demers in 2005—appears like a tidier, fully evergreen version of its Asian counterpart akebia. It has recently been determined that this is the first plant species to

exhibit mimetic polymorphism, a fancy way of saying that in the wilds of Chile its foliage changes form depending on the host tree it is growing in.

Another revelation: as a nurseryman, I cannot think of a more despicable assemblage of plants to cultivate than those that twine. This may explain precisely why so many acceptable and distinctive vining plants are hard to find. A flat of perfectly behaved vining, twining seedlings will dreadlock themselves to one another overnight. Wrestling just one from a flat becomes a fool's errand. They are independent-minded, strong-willed, and clever creatures that I would not be without—but I would rather have someone else grow them for me.

The Terrace

AFTER GARDENING ON THE SITE for three years, removing turf and establishing the bluff garden, I was keenly aware of one truth. Despite the fact that we could see an expanse of Puget Sound arcing from the northeast to the southwest, and that the haunting laugh of migrating loons, screeching bald eagles, barking sea lions, and mournful foghorns were part of our daily audibles, the property was delusively dry. Even on overcast days—that would be

The foliage of *Holboellia yaoshanensis* might aptly be described as seductive.

on average 308 days per year—the bluff was hot and thirsty. Puget Sound was nothing more than a distant mirage.

As the construction of the house was nearing completion, the hardscape of the garden was drafted on drawing paper. We needed to bring the shoreline up the bluff to the house itself. To accomplish this, we designed a series of pools and falls and rills to embrace the terrace and provide a buffer between the impression of an oasis and the drier land below.

Large boulders were hand selected and placed to create the bones of the water features. Gravel-amended planting pockets among the rocks and concrete would create beneficial micro sites and heat sinks for plants that I would not normally be able to cultivate successfully.

Virtually any new water feature will appear out of place and artificial—especially those designed to be natural in appearance. Forethought of the inclusion of as many planting sites as possible at the edge of the concrete or liner

Looking up the Lutyens-inspired stairs to the south side of the dining alcove and the surrounding terrace, you can see water features on the left.

Rills are the emotional and physical buffer between the bluff and the more lived-in terrace.

is important. Though the edges of the entirety of the water features outside of the connecting rills are surfaced with a graveled mortar, two low-growing evergreen cotoneasters—*Cotoneaster horizontalis* collected in China in 1996 and *C. microphyllus* var. *cochleatus* from eastern Nepal in 1995 and again in 2002—have proven to be the ultimate darn.

Here too, in sunny dry pockets along the water's edge I have included a perennial morning glory, *Convolulus sabatius*, that presents perpetual blue flowering along its trailing stems, which mitigate in a pleasing way the harsh edge of which we speak. Nearby, a dwarf wisteria received by J. C. Raulston—what species it belongs to is still a conundrum, but it is presumably *Wisteria floribunda*—acts as a well-behaved small tree and lends seasonal interest.

Another champion is a North African subshrub in the daisy family known as *Rhodanthemum atlanticum*. This plant came to me by way of Panayoti Kelaidis, a longtime friend and accomplished horticulturist at the Denver Botanic Gardens. This small silver-gray-foliaged evergreen begins presenting prideful white daisies often as early as late January, not only bringing me a great sense of elation at seeing such delicate things do battle with sometimes brutal nighttime temperatures but also reminding me of how much influence Panayoti has had on my life as a gardener. Among the many heroes in horticulture I have had the opportunity to interface with, he stands alone in his accomplishment of turning his passion into one of the world's most remarkable gardens while possessing an enviable, unsurpassed eloquence.

Concave boulders would hold water for bathing birds, skinks, snakes, and rodents. I would have koi in the pools, and swallows would skim the surface for water. Frogs would come to lay their eggs and sing loudly in March and April,

ABOVE LEFT · When the terrace and water features were under construction in 2004, as shown here, initial planting of the bluff had already commenced. Not a single plant was disturbed or damaged during the fifteen-month construction process.

A view of the lower water feature looking toward the terrace shows the convex boulders used in the terrace construction, the suturing by cotoneaster, and the dwarf wisteria in spring.

I hoped. And I knew that the notes and octaves of kinetic molecules of water would be in harmony, or at least conjure the movement of Puget Sound against the shoreline two hundred feet below our bluff. The sound of the sound would be directly outside of our door. The small pools would become avatars of the great tidal forces beyond, providing depth and transparency while gathering the goings-on above their mirrored surfaces. Yet often in garden creation, what one hopes to achieve is augmented by things unexpected.

I knew that I wanted to continue the stained concrete flooring material used indoors out onto the terrace, where the dark color would absorb the heat during the day, while cut lines shared from inside to outside would seamlessly suture the terrace to the interior.

The oases were created as I had hoped. They settled and thrived in what I was certain was record time. The juxtaposition of arid and moist, the tension between those two conditions only inches apart, is emphasized with *Opuntia* blossoms virtually hanging into the water. *Chamaerops humilis*, *Butia capitata*, *Trachycarpus fortunei*, and *Sabal palmetto* deliver parched visual cues, though all of these palms are much more tolerant of winter wet than most believe. One of several hardy bromeliads, *Ochagavia carnea*, and the tender *Correa* 'Federation Belle' thrive in the heat sink provided by the concrete terrace and nearby rocks. *Fascicularia pitcairnifolia*, an epiphytic bromeliad from Chile, is perfectly at home as a terrestrial given sufficient heat and good drainage.

ABOVE · *Fascicularia pitcairnifolia* is an epiphytic bromeliad that is perfectly at home in the ground given enough heat and drainage.

ABOVE RIGHT · *Ochagavia carnea*, a hardy bromeliad, thrives in the terrace heat sink.

OPPOSITE TOP · The infinity-edge pool on the terrace brings to our doorstep an echo of Puget Sound beyond, in peace or in tantrum.

OPPOSITE · Looking south to the upper fire pit provides a view of the arresting beauty of *Arctostaphylos densiflora* 'Howard McMinn' on the terrace.

Banksia integrifolia subsp. *monticola*, sited on the terrace directly outside of the master bedroom, produces hummingbird-attracting, nectar-rich flowers from October through March and provides a repeat platform for nesting Anna's hummingbirds, easily observed through the bedroom window. Grevilleas from Australia blossom unperturbed, and, along with the *Correa*, feed the hummingbirds throughout winter.

On the western end of the terrace, it was my sincere intention to recreate a bog of my youth. In an enormous cement bathtub adjacent to a waterfall and rill would be found, in my dreams, *Saracennia* and sundews, *Kalmia*, and *Ledum*,

all aided by the extra heat offered by the surrounding darkly dyed concrete, transporting me back to the effervescent explorations of youth. The result, however, is a far cry from anything naturally occurring in my home state.

My "unnatural" bog was just one of the many things I did not anticipate when excitedly gazing at the neat but quickly designed terrace that Robert so expertly drew on the drafting paper. Birds would come to the concave pools to bathe in droves, a joy to witness—but not a joy to clean up after. Koi would thrive in my pool and come when I fed them—but river otters, raccoons, and herons, too, discovered the joys of an oasis in the Pacific Northwest. It might be of interest to note that precisely as I was writing the previous sentence, I was alerted by our dogs that the sleek, long-bodied, furry leviathan had returned to polish off a population of tiny White Cloud minnows I had firmly established as hardy controllers of mosquito larvae.

And I soon discovered that the sound of a waterfall at night is more easily tolerated by a forty-five-year-old than by a sixty-five-year-old. And agaves, if well grown and content, become freakishly large.

These are but minor details. I still love the terrace, mostly. I enjoy walking on the warm concrete at night in my socks. I relish watching the moon reflected in Puget Sound, which is in turn reflected in the pools. And I rejoice in the sound of frogs in March and April.

However, the most profound lesson garnered is that the terrace, with its rills and pools and falls, does not at all connect the bluff garden to the house. It does precisely the opposite. Right at our doorstep, it creates a barrier, a perch we always go to but less frequently go beyond. The garden below, in

ABOVE · *Banksia integrifolia* subsp. *monticola* attracts hummingbirds from October through March.

ABOVE RIGHT · *Grevillea* 'Canberra Gem' blossoms for eight months of the year.

OPPOSITE · *Correa* 'Federation Belle' is tender but performs admirably with the heat provided by the concrete terrace and nearby rocks.

THE HOUSE AND TERRACE

The bog was meant to recreate a landscape of my youth, yet the resulting congregation of wet-loving plants from across the globe is quite unlike any bog I have witnessed anywhere I have traveled.

all of its astounding growth and color and fragrance and movement, has not become a place that eagerly beckons to be explored as I had hoped it would. The Lutyens-inspired steps do not implicitly extend an invitation to step over the barrier to see what more there is to see. Instead the terrace has become my laboratory, a place to perfect my points of admiration from a distance. The bluff beyond is a canvas on which to, without great finesse, smear copious quantities of chromatic impressionism.

The terrace is not a failure, nor is it a success. It is pleasing. I suppose to some it is annoying. It simply did not come to serve what I had imagined its purpose would be.

ABOVE · A great blue heron takes flight from the infinity pool after hastily inspecting the quickly diminishing population of surviving koi.

ABOVE LEFT · Koi initially thrived in our pools until discovered by river otters that obliterated their much-adored presence in the garden virtually overnight.

Cactus and Succulents

DUBLIN'S HELEN DILLON, arguably one of Europe's best-known hands-on gardeners and first lady of the British Isle's horticultural cognoscenti, once queried during a lecture I was attending, "Why is it that Americans don't use more cactus in their gardens? After all," she continued, "they are from the New World and the texture they provide is unparalleled by any other assemblage of plants."

As I began planting Windcliff, I took Dillon's words to heart and began to collect and trial as many hardy species of cactus and other succulents as possible in our sharply well-drained glacial till, blasted by full sun—as much as the Pacific Northwest climate can possibly blast in that regard. I honed the drainage further by integrating pea gravel and grit into the beds of the terrace as well as appending a five-inch stratum of weathered amber-colored quartz to

Opuntia phaeacantha dips its pads into the infinity pool on the terrace alongside *Aloiampelos striatula* (formerly *Aloe striatula*).

the top of the beds before planting to preserve the rot-sensitive crowns of the drought-loving plants.

The area under the overhanging eaves on the south side of the house, generally possessing an edaphic complexion as inviting as the surface of Mars, has become the perfect niche for plants requiring more precise watering regimes and moderated temperatures. If provided unabridged dryness during the coldest months, even the tenderest species are likely to succeed.

When I sheltered *Neobuxbaumia polylopha* from Mexico as well as *Echinopsis pachanoi* from Argentina in the corner of the house outside the dining room, both as young plants less than six inches high, I was obviously devoid of any optimism that either would actually thrive. The former is now seven feet high while the latter is four; thrusting their spiny-ribbed, terrorist-inspired columns skyward, they appear more a threat against humanity and an ode to illogical planting design than things of beauty. I will allow the next owner of this property to deal with the problem.

The deserts of the world—whether the Galapagos or Death Valley—detonate with color when rains return to the parched landscape. In North and South America, much of this color comes from cacti when a steady progression of ephemeral satiny flowers appear in soft yellows, reds, and corals, all on a framework with a formidable attitude. In a practical gardening sense, this means that in a climate with moderate or even heavy amounts of natural precipitation, flowering will occur every year, an event in midsummer that I have come to anticipate as eagerly as the first blossoming hellebores of February.

Note: These plants that have adapted to survive where few other plants can, do not suffer lightly consumption of their embodiment by potential grazers. Species with large spines offer visual appeal—from a safe distance—as their needle-y armor bleaches and holds the light. However, even if a cactus appears spineless, a more insidious defense system may be present in the form of glochids. These tiny, barely visible barbs surpass all other known annoyances and become noticeable between your fingers at roughly 2 a.m. Synthetic, puncture-resistant gloves and a four-dollar fish hook puller from any sporting goods department provide protection. And, as a dog owner, I must mention that while canines quickly fathom the concept of spines, they do not associate the delayed distress of glochids with the plants they are rumbling on. Site those species carefully or simply avoid them entirely.

Aloe barbadensis, aka aloe vera, a tender succulent houseplant with gelatinous sap that can be dabbed, swabbed, smeared, or swallowed for every known human malady, was my entrée to a rather large assemblage of additional species native to Africa. We cultivate only a handful of hardy aloe in the garden at Windcliff, but it is a handful worth growing.

Neobuxbaumia polylopha and *Echinopsis pachanoi*, along with an assortment of aloes, do fine in a sheltered bed beneath the eaves of the house.

Agave salmiana has gained a
stature I did not expect, thriving
between a rock and a hard place on
the terrace, literally.

The once rare spiral aloe, *Aloe polyphylla*, whose vortex of foliage unfurls
in either a clockwise or a counterclockwise direction depending on the genetics of the individual seedling, is a remarkably hardy species, tolerating temperatures as low as 10 degrees F if provided a sharply draining soil. Branched
stems capped by tubular orange flowers appear in early summer after the plant
reaches sexual maturity, though my specimens at Windcliff are shy to blossom.
Foolproof *Aloe aristata*, recently reclassified as *Aristaloe*, also sheltering beneath
our south-facing eaves, provides durable evergreen rosettes with dependable
bright orange, nectar-rich flowers in early spring.

One of the hardiest of the caulescent or stemmed aloes, *Aloiampelos striatula* (formerly *Aloe striatula*) will tolerate winter moisture as long as the soil
is fast draining. My plants have been killed to the ground repeatedly during an

ABOVE · *Aristaloe aristata* blooms bright orange in early spring.

ABOVE RIGHT · *Aloe polyphylla* is remarkably hardy in sharply draining soil.

OPPOSITE · *Cylindropuntia fulgida*, the so-called jumping cholla, features dense spines that are best appreciated from a safe distance.

extremely wet and cold winter but quickly sprang back to form handsome compact mounds. Fleshy elongate leaves are carried along multiple vertical canes to three and a half feet with erect racemes of orange, fading to yellow, tubular flowers in spring and then, as the days shorten, once again in September and early October.

The thin light-green leaves of *Aloe cooperi*, one of the so-called grass aloes, emerge in spring, rising to fifteen inches with a very kniphofia-like growth habit. This species performs well in a beefier soil than one might expect. In our garden, simple racemes of pretty orange tubular flowers appear from late summer into early winter, generally on the latter side.

Containers

POT GARDENING is now fully legal in Washington State, yet savvy gardeners have been practitioners of the craft for centuries. Containerized plants were the gateway drug for most of the horticulturally obsessed of my generation. Embarrassingly, I still possess two of my original houseplants. In the event you might think me a caring and devoted flower child of the sixties, know that these are two I could easily have left in a closet for a decade—or two—and they still would have survived.

One of my first houseplants, *Fockea edulis*, a caudiciform in the milk-weed family from Africa, continues to thrive through my neglect. My parents adopted the other, *Maranta leuconeura*, when I left for college. Its general welfare seemed to be the only thing they could agree on, so as a reminder of that rare treaty I re-adopted it after their departures. Both of these venerable plants spend their summers on the terrace and vacation during the winter in the dining room. Those two, along with *Clivia*, which I have raised from seed

THIS SPREAD · *Cylindropuntia ramosissima* (syn. *Opuntia ramosissima*), *Agave albopilosa*, and *Crassula capitella* spend summers on the terrace and winters in the greenhouse.

A potted collection of
assorted succulents,
cacti, and dwarf
Eucomis resides in sum-
mer on the terrace.

The dwarf *Eucomis*
'Leia' produces its pink
pineapple-like blossoms
throughout summer.

and which blossoms dependably for me all winter along the southern wall of the hall, are the only true houseplants I tend.

The rest of the terrace "pottery" consists primarily of plants that can be maintained in our cold greenhouse. These include an ever-rotating inventory of succulents whose lives would be endangered if exposed to our lowest temperatures and normal winter rainfall, including arborescent forms of *Sedum* and *Oxalis*, *Delosperma*, *Agave*, *Aloe*, caudiciform *Pelargonium*, *Crassula*, *Echeveria*, and assorted cacti. Those familiar with the watering requirement of any one of these genera knows the watering regimen of the entire lot. These containers look good all summer long. I water them when I get around to it, and they all like the added heat provided by sitting on dark-stained concrete.

Somewhat more demanding are the *Eucomis* specimens that I keep potted for a better display in blossom and the species *Gladiolus* that eventually diminish in the garden. The genus *Eucomis* is fully hardy in the Pacific Northwest, but the more diminutive species and hybrids would be lost in my botanical sea of agitation. They make superlative container plants, remaining effective for years without repotting. I simply add a bit of fertilizer in spring and begin watering the containers in June. They are in full foliage by the Fourth of July and present weeks of pineapple-inspired spikes of flowers in a rich assortment of colors throughout July into September. I cannot say enough good things about their ratio of ease to enjoyment.

A couple container caveats. Agaves are sharp—cutting the tips from their leaves on a regular basis can prevent a ruinous evening with finely attired guests. Some of the aloes, in particular *Aloe greatheadii*, a stupendously dependable blossoming species, produce early flowers on stems to four feet, beckoning hummingbirds into the greenhouse where the birds cannot easily escape. We bring the aloes outside before flowers commence to prevent this unintended invitation that can end in tragedy.

Above all, select a good vessel. Though my tastes run to unglazed simple forms, they need not be costly Italian or Anduze terracotta. My favorites are Long Toms that cost less than twelve dollars apiece. The pots should be convex (flared outward), not concave, if you have plans ever to transplant the contents. Consider the style and color of the containers—not the plants in them— as the unifying element. I prefer to leave a generous amount of headspace in each pot and top-dress with fine grit to prevent weeds and spillage of the soil medium during watering.

The Pot Wall

Diminutive and precious plants congregate in the pot wall, a botanical wonderland directly outside the kitchen door.

A striking container display at the entry to our house was inspired by a chance encounter coupled with the utter failure to launch of our initial approach. While I was visiting a vastly entertaining and plant-savvy garden in Mississippi, Hayes Jackson shared with me his approach to growing plants with differing edaphic requirements side by side. This was achieved by planting in remnants of a dismantled brick chimney that had individual flues still intact. Each hollow flue was filled with precisely the correct soil mix for each plant, and the result was smart in its ruinous appearance.

I now enter into evidence a true story that will show with no degree of uncertainty my complete fraudulency and naiveté with regard to design.

At Heronswood, our dogs, Chico and Collé, were walked up our driveway each morning to the office, where they spent their days annoying customers and employees alike. In the evening, they returned by the same route and after dinner were taken out to romp and roll on the small lawn we maintained. The treasures of the woodland were left to thrive unfettered by paws and lifted legs.

Overflowing with delusions of grandeur and my godlike status in making woodland plants thrive, I mindlessly employed a four-foot-wide stretch of earth along the north side of our house at Windcliff, directly outside of the pantry door, to grow the wonders I had cut my teeth on as a younger man in my first garden. Never for a moment did I consider the traffic patterns and

marking behaviors of our beloved canines. It was as if I had lined up my favorite delicacies along a wall and then handed an assault weapon to each dog as they asked to be let out.

Our solution was slightly more upscale than repurposed rubble but not that far off the mark. Robert found a local source for very inexpensive unstained glass-fiber-reinforced cement containers in varying heights and widths. Mindful of plugged drainage holes, we hammered the entire bottom out of each container. After staining the pots, we began the rather entertaining process of puzzling the pots together to form a wall of varying height and depth.

To avoid soil compaction inherent to container culture, I went heavy on mineral components, mixing #6 sandblasting grit half and half with my standard custom-blended nursery potting mix, which also contains additional pumice to resist compaction. During the planting process, based on assessing the individual needs of each plant incorporated into the wall, I amended the soil mix with lime, peat, or additional gravel.

Thrilled by the cessation of lifted legs each morning, plants in the pot wall have thrived. These include *Maianthemum oleraceum*, a handsome and vigorous false Solomon's seal that is both graceful in habit and sensational in flower and fruit, collected in northern Myanmar in 2013; a particularly good form of *Arisaema consanguineum* with impressively long drip tips

collected in Arunachal Pradesh in 2016; and *Begonia grandis* 'Heron's Pirouette', a selection made at Heronswood in the mid-1990s. *Paris rugosa*, a diminutive species collected in Yunnan in 1996, would not stand a chance in the open ground but thrives to a superlative degree in the pot wall.

The dogs, initially perplexed by the lack of scolding for performing basic bodily functions, are content to walk around, not through, the planting.

And the intricacies of each flower and leaf are brought closer to the eye for clearer admiration. Fully satisfied with the results, we are doubling the wall in length during the writing of this text.

CLOCKWISE FROM LEFT ·
*Paris rugosa, Arisaema consan-
guineum, Maianthemum oleraceum*

OPPOSITE · *Begonia grandis*
'Heron's Pirouette'

The
Potager

Long before my degrees and professional felicitations, before all the commotion over GMOs and organic certification, before I even knew what a potager was or considered attempting to make one handsome, I was first a proud vegetable gardener—and still am. In my youth, the turf of a new vegetable garden was still turned by plough, and when the soil had dried sufficiently in spring, a lavish straw-based topping of cow poop and lime was roto-tilled in. Year upon year afterward, following a contemptibly long winter and hungered-for thaw came the intoxicating scent of cool, gritty loam between my fingers. I smell it still.

The potager at Windcliff consists of raised beds surrounding the greenhouse and large containers for ease of maintenance and harvest. We eat well from this space twelve months of the year.

First a Vegetable Gardener

I DON'T EVEN REMEMBER why I thirsted so badly to be a vegetable gardener. My parents were raised on no-nonsense shelled peas and honest potatoes from their own backyards, the growing of which was nothing more than a chore they were eager to abandon as adults. That bottle of magic filled with the marvels of weeding a row of germinating carrots or seeing beans lift the soil on their shoulders had for them emptied years earlier. We had no vegetable garden before my own; instead iceberg lettuce and cans of corn and peas served as adventure guides in the kitchen. My parents would have starved with a trug

As an MSU Spartan, I was compelled to include the eponymous apple in our small orchard. One tree provides us a full year's supply of sauce and pies.

full of plump fennel bulbs and bunches of freshly harvested basil, parsley, and cilantro on the counter. They would have been irritated by fresh spinach.

So of all the things I have done in my gardening career, most of it cleverly ripped off and rebranded, vegetable gardening has been the solo journey. Germinating seeds of gourds was my own unpatented discovery.

In 1980, upon moving to the Wenatchee Valley, a comestibles paradise, I became proficient at preserving and pickling. In 1988, at Heronswood, after realizing the absence of soil between the rocks we rototilled, we installed simple raised beds on the east side of the house. We consumed admirably from those boxes, including rhubarb pies from divisions of a great uncle's plant I had carried westward across the Great Plains in my Pontiac Sunbird. Yet there was no inspiration beyond eating well and, well, cheaply. After all, I was raised a Lutheran. Lutherans don't buy onion sets. They sow onion seed.

BELOW · The perennial herbs, including sage and rosemary, are grown only steps from the kitchen.

BELOW RIGHT · "Know your onions" is an expression we take literally. Through trial and error, we have come to rely on the best keepers in our climate, including Cortland. It has been decades since we last purchased an onion in a grocery store.

Taste Makers

ALREADY, IN THE EARLY 1990S, Heronswood had become the loom that began to weave our lives into a novel fabric of celebrated plantsmen and designers. During our first Grand Tour of English Gardens, we were guests of Rosemary Verey at Barnsley House and Christopher Lloyd at Great Dixter, and we found a warm hearth with Nori and Sandra Pope at Hadspen House.

We returned intoxicated by notions of what was good, better, and best to grow in our potager—we had, as you will notice, already commenced calling it a potager. Our consideration became growing it in a manner beyond rows and rectangles and, most important, preparing our harvests more creatively. Even today, we continue to prepare meals from recipes copied from Christo's mother's cookbook, though we have never perfected the art of forcing Belgium endive in our wine cellar. Not having a wine cellar may be at the root of this failure.

Joe Eck and Wayne Winterrowd, of the inestimable garden called North Hill in Readsboro, Vermont, traveled the same circuits, and we were often guests in their home. Somehow, they did everything bigger and better than we did. And they knew it. With a clarified style and menu, their kitchen infused us with inspiration and frequent irritation. Never was a rutabaga so precious.

ABOVE · Our interest in exploring new varietals migrates from genera to genera each year, with a surfeit of our chosen crop of exploration. Still, there are never enough vine-ripened tomatoes, with the excess turned to sauce and canned.

ABOVE LEFT · Tomatoes must be cultivated inside the greenhouse, as the chill of Puget Sound at night during the summer leads to late blight rather early.

Wayne would frequently write me fifteen-page letters to report the weather, but before each letter culminated in the predicted low temperatures they would soon be brutalized by, he would share with me his newest source for the best squash varieties one could possibly grow, and intriguing ways to prepare them. I was never sure if he actually was preparing them that way or simply thinking that he might someday, but his letters frequently made our kitchen smell like a kitchen should.

In 1994, after we jettisoned the original vegetable garden at Heronswood in lieu of perennial borders, Robert laid out the potager to the west of our house. John van den Meerendonk executed the stonework to perfection; together, John and I had led the team at Bloedel Reserve when Robert and I lived there in the mid-1980s. The square parterre held four outer and four inner beds, each edged in dwarf box. The perimeter plantings were done up in saucy colors by my friend and right-hand man Duane West (and are still maintained by him now in the same ambitious fashion under the new reiteration of Heronswood). Heronista Darrah Cole must be credited for planting and tending the potager during that time, as I was on a plane more often than in the soil.

When Heronswood was shuttered and we removed ourselves entirely to Windcliff in 2006, for the first time since fifth grade I was without a vegetable garden, and for the first time in nearly two decades without a greenhouse and potting bench. Not fully realizing the magnitude of these absences, for two years I was crippled emotionally.

The Greenhouse and Raised Beds

IN 2009 WE CONSTRUCTED a twenty-by-sixty-foot greenhouse on a site that guaranteed the best vantage of daylong sun—a surprisingly tall order for a six-and-a-half-acre south-facing bluffside property where mature trees thrived in precisely all the wrong locations. Sadly, we had to sacrifice a mature and healthy Pacific dogwood, *Cornus nuttallii*, to make things fit.

Raised beds constructed of cement blocks clad with clear cedar planks surround the glasshouse's east, south, and west sides, where sufficient sunlight insolates in the morning and evening to satisfy the solar requirements of crops against the adjacent greenhouse walls.

The west side of the greenhouse proved to be the sunniest and warmest, so it was here that we created an allée bordered by more raised beds. By complete serendipity, I stumbled upon a closeout sale at an industrial container supply outlet

Babu inspects the pumpkin patch with a ripening cache of 'Winter Luxury', a pie pumpkin so delectable and with such keeping qualities that legislation should demand its presence in every garden. Seen in the distance just behind Babu is the Andean yacón, *Smallanthus sonchifolius*, which produces an incredible haul of sweet-potato-like tubers that we harvest as needed throughout the winter.

where I found large-scaled containers at prices we could afford. The durable fiberglass pots coated with a ferrous-impregnated grit have weathered well and effectively gather warmth. In the winter, greens are rotated continually through the containers, and later in the year some of the more varmint-vulnerable summer crops are kept safely away from pairs of prominent incisors.

Concrete slabs meant to hold the large vessels were poured in place and stained dark brown to better absorb the heat. At first we surrounded them with large-diameter beach rock, a repeat of the infill surrounding identical concrete pads placed along the north and west sides of the house, where the texture is effective. The large rocks made for sincerely mean walking in what had become one of the most uninviting potagers created since serpent-infested Eden itself. It was undeniably the worst miscalculation I've made thus far in my journey at Windcliff, other than the time I pruned a tree while listening to the Mariners blow a twelve-run lead in the bottom of the eighth.

Shortly thereafter, reflective terracotta-colored crushed brick replaced the beach rock, which was repurposed to create gabion walls defining the space reserved for fruit trees and soft fruits. It was a happy day when my profound and mindless blunder was fully rectified.

For a measure of good luck and domestic tranquility, *Nandina domestica* is planted at the entrance to the potager and adjoining greenhouse.

On the north end, to partition the potager from the nursery beyond, Robert constructed a façade that provides a framework for three torch-cut sheet-steel storyboards executed by Berkeley, California, artist Mark Bulwinkle. One depicts Robert's Northwest roots and his time in the Navy, another shows me in Michigan surrounded by snowflakes and mosquitoes, and a third is of Robert and me square dancing in Seattle with my beloved dog, Emerson, bordered by hearts and musical notes. The pieces have developed a patina that closely matches the row of giant urns nearby. The structure also offers support for an espaliered fig and provides trellises for peas and beans.

ABOVE · Large ceramic and surprisingly comely fiberglass containers are positioned on concrete slabs that are stained dark brown to better absorb heat. In these, after the soil is enriched with compost, crops are rotated throughout the year.

RIGHT · The central storyboard, created by Berkeley, California, artist Mark Bulwinkle, celebrates Robert's and my introduction to one another while square dancing in Seattle in 1983.

The soil in the potager is amended and replenished annually with our own compost along with horse manure from local farms that use sawdust rather than straw. A fertilizer blend based on Steve Solomon's recipe in his exceptional book *The Intelligent Gardener: Growing Nutrient-Dense Food* is applied at a rate of six quarts per hundred square feet each spring. Our barely modified recipe:

> cottonseed meal (2 parts)
> rock phosphate (1 part)
> kelp meal (1 part)
> fish meal (1 part)
> agricultural lime (¼ part)
> agricultural gypsum (¼ part)
> feather meal (¼ part)

Excess mix is kept in a garbage can to reapply, more sparsely, when new crops are rotated throughout the year. Note that feather and fish meal can attract varmints, including canines that will take great delight in romping between freshly planted rows of beans to which it has been applied.

The potager is never as perfect and productive as I want it to be. Cabbages swell to beach ball size one year and fail to even establish the next. Dill refuses to grow when we have good crops of cucumbers and grows lavishly when there are no cukes to pick. But the potager feeds us well, and it feels good to be within. The greenhouse ripens tomatoes, peppers, and (sometimes) cucumbers for pickling. We feast on fresh asparagus until we have had our fill and freeze the excess for winter soups. Onions, garlic, pumpkins, and squashes carry us through winter and beyond, squeezing by with marginal quality before the new harvest begins. Beets and beans are pickled; salsa and tomato sauce are canned.

And as each crop is planted, weeded, and harvested, I smell the soil between my fingers and beneath my nails and reaffirm that yearning to be, above all else, a vegetable gardener.

Having the first ripened tomato on the block remains as proud an accomplishment for me at sixty-six years of age as it was at age seven. I simply have more social platforms on which to brag about it now.

Eating Through the Calendar

Eating something from our garden every day of the year, which we do, is neither magical nor novel. We maintain a heady collection of hardneck and softneck garlic selections—at last count, more than twenty-seven—that are planted in early October. Their flower scapes are harvested for roasting in early summer and the bulbs lifted by early August. Their removal gives ample room for autumn and winter crops, including a late sowing of beans, winter cauliflower, and different strains of sprouting broccoli from which we will harvest throughout the winter.

Kale is established in early spring and continues to offer fresh, tender leaves throughout the following winter. Onions—many seed strains—are sown by seed in January and harvested in early September, though we use immature bulbs as one might employ scallions as we thin their rows in early summer.

Though leeks are left in the ground throughout the winter and harvested as needed, the onions, shallots, and garlic join the squashes and pumpkins in our cool but dry garage, which has become by default our root cellar. Just as I did during my infancy as a gardener of edibles, we leave parsnips in the ground to harvest throughout the winter months when their sugars have fully developed.

Swiss chard provides a good cooked green during the coldest and darkest months, though our first crops of spinach are generally ready to harvest by late February if the stars align.

Mesclun is sown in flats in our unheated seed frames and then brought into the greenhouse to mature after germination, and is cut for salads from November through March; the salad operation then fully retreats back into the raised beds in mid-February.

Perennial crops, including a nonbolting variety of sorrel, rhubarb, asparagus, and horseradish are obviously left in the same place from year to year, while all other crops are rotated as much as one can rotate on a small plot. Both dill and arugula are left standing until their seeds are mature, as they find their own niche more effectively than I could.

Factoring time and materials, no one is going to save money on a vegetable garden any more than they will make money raising chickens for eggs. Yet if one considers the distilled pleasure of eating fresh vegetables within minutes of harvest, a plot or pot of any size devoted to edibles makes for a much wealthier, healthier life.

Pumpkins and squashes from the garden are brought in to cure for a week near the AGA stove in our kitchen, significantly extending their keeping quality.

The Nursery

Do this for me. Place a seed, the tiniest you can find, that of a hydrangea or begonia or giant sequoia, singly upon your thumb. Now hold it up to the light to inspect it more closely. Yes, you may use your reading glasses. There, beneath its seed coat, the lion's share of its mass is simply stored energy in the form of starch or fat. But inside that speck upon your thumb is also found the embryo, a tiny mass of cells that can when awakened destroy concrete, melt hearts, and provide the stuff of honey. Having watched countless times the ignition of life in a germinating seed, having bumbled my way into the arcade of growing plants for a living, I remain grateful and fulfilled.

A cart of Windcliff-grown plants, ostensibly on their way to market, sits idly in the nursery.

My Raison d'Etre

I BEGAN MY LIFE in the world that I occupy by planting a seed, and I would gratefully come to the end of my life while planting yet more seed. It is a fascination I was born to and undoubtedly will keep with me to my final days.

If the definition of a nursery is an enterprise where plants are produced in excess of the mother plant, then by default, anyone who gardens has a nursery. Those who cannot bring themselves to compost any reasonably healthy surplus—the fruit of any garden—begins the accumulation of treasures and trinkets for gifts and trade. Politely dubbed the holding area, this jumble of oftentimes half-living, thirsty plants in recycled plastic containers choked with weeds represents, in actuality, the protean nursery. The weak or the obsessed allow it to morph to uncontrollable proportions, ultimately leading to mercenary methods of dispersal. Gratifyingly, those who hone techniques to do just that may possibly recoup up to, but seldom exceeding, a full quarter of its value in time, energy, and materials invested.

The generator of esoteric biomass, the grower of groove, the specialty nursery is nothing more than a simple farmer with a twist, as the prickly challenges are precisely the same: fickle and demanding consumers, unpredictable weather, and nonexistent profit margins. Yet surprisingly, every year there are new players on the field. If the foundation is a true passion for plants, the textural differences one from another are more or less indecipherable, no matter what the specialty actually is, no matter how large or small. In the end, all gardeners are nurserypeople, but not all nurserypeople are necessarily gardeners. Beware those who serve fare they will not eat themselves.

Despite the complexities and vagaries, I can't imagine *not* having a nursery, so I began the process again after two tortuous years without, following the shuttering of Heronswood. From 2006 until I returned to Heronswood to rejoin old friends in 2012, much of what I grew was the result of seed gathered during my biyearly trips abroad. Those six years became by far my most productive in collection work.

Simply finding a sought-after species in the wild far from guarantees that you have a bird in hand. Can you reach it hanging precariously from a cliff? Does it have ripened seed? Has the seed been parasitized? Should it not get lost in the mail, will it pass inspection by the USDA? Will it germinate? Will it survive transplanting? It took three trips to the same high plateau near Zhongdian (since renamed Shangri-la), Yunnan Province, and scouring the massive population of *Euphorbia jalkinii* that paints the landscape an outrageous, glowing red in autumn, to find at last a paltry number of viable fruit. From that successful collection in 2000, I have my own autumn display at Windcliff while also appreciating the charms of its springtime chartreuse flowers. We began to distribute the plant in 2007 from Windcliff.

Once again, bearing witness to the lifting of the soil in late winter and early spring, signaling erumpent embryos we have cajoled for months or years, remains no less alluring to me than a weeklong seminar in charms and spells at Hogworts. There might be nothing more exciting for this gardener's soul than to discover that a plant I have long hoped to grow is at last presenting itself, often in duplicate with the potential for a variation on a theme.

Within (nearly) every pot, three or a hundred or five hundred individuals emerge from seeds I have extracted by smushing or drying fruit on trails or in musty hotel rooms, each individual possessing a portent of its very own. Each of the three or a hundred or five hundred seedlings, though of the same species, will express to the world its unique identity.

Through trial and error, we have arrived at what we believe is the best general sowing medium for taxa that we anticipate will take a considerable time to germinate, high in fine grit to avoid compaction and add aeration. A visit to the seed frames in spring can be as anticipatory as checking on wrapped presents under the tree. Numerous taxa take up to three years to germinate, requiring maintenance of the pot for a considerable time before we conclude that the sowing of the seed was for naught.

Though there may be some discernible differences among seedlings as early as the cotyledon stage—for instance, variegated seedlings emerge with a variegated seed leaf—much of the variability we hope to find by growing so many seedlings begins after transplanting the young plants to liners. Intriguing individuals are then cherry picked and planted out into the garden, and the waiting game begins in anticipation of inaugural flowering.

Obviously, available space becomes an issue during the process. Sadly, not every seedling is allowed the opportunity to fulfill its destiny, and I shudder to think how many excellent garden plants have been composted in the culling of excess. How many of those were the keepers?

We wait for the first flowers unrequitedly, wondering precisely what genetics we happened upon and captured in a clean line of seed at the bottom of a glassine envelope at a trip's end. How much will these individuals differ from the expectations offered in the floras of the regions from which they come? Relax. Probably not much.

But during that wait, the hope that this spring will be *the* spring that the characteristics of the plant I have been watering, fertilizing, pruning, talking to, and cussing at for five, fifteen, or twenty years will at last be revealed is the hope that carries me through winter. In the autumn of 2018, plump flower buds appeared on *Magnolia campbellii* (northeastern Nepal, 2002) and blossomed

ABOVE · *Euphorbia jalkinii* DJHC 0176 is now distributed from Windcliff after I made three trips to the same high plateau in Yunnan Province to find viable seed.

TOP · My good friend Jennifer Macuiba accompanied me to remote eastern Nepal in 1995. Helping to dry and sort our seed collections, she is also double-checking our collection data while awaiting our flight from the airstrip in Tumlingtar back to Kathmandu for seed inspection, after which they will be dispatched to the USDA for additional inspection.

RIGHT · Seedling pots in the nursery are carefully labeled with names and collection data in anticipation of their eventual germination.

BELOW · Two siblings of the same parent of *Schefflera taiwaniana* collected in Taiwan in 2007 illuminate the potential for enormous genetic variation held within seeds.

The greenhouse and
seed frames in spring
are where charms and
spells unfold.

the following spring for the first time. I was gobsmacked. I am still irascibly waiting for collections of *Aesculus wangii* (Vietnam, 2003) and *Carpinus fangiana* (China, 2008) to put up or shut up. In this frustrating, marvelous, priceless postponement, I wish for everyone to have at least one plant in his or her garden that has not yet flowered. Once it has, the gift wrapping is off.

Windcliff Plants

IT IS WHEN YOU BEGIN collecting seed in your own garden where you have brought together under unnatural circumstances a cluster of first cousins who have never met, that things become tantalizing. By moth, hummingbird, butterfly, bee, and sometimes paintbrush, pollen is immodestly shared from species to species, and the likelihood of weird children playing banjoes is enhanced.

I have taken the lazy man's approach to selecting unnatural pairings from this entourage originating in far-flung locales. Others, profoundly more talented than I will ever be, seek out the raw data for the express purpose of recombining the best to make something better. Of all the gardeners and nurserymen I have met, John Massey of Ashwood Nursery in the United Kingdom ranks among the gods in dreaming of plants that are yet to be—frenetically and meticulously gathering all their genetic potentialities and turning out for our pleasure things of wonder. There are others similarly talented. I remain indebted to their dedication to the craft as well as light years behind in capability.

The nursery at Windcliff is far from sustainable. There is no business plan. Still, I continue to produce and distribute plants and somehow imagine that I am making enough income to justify the effort. However, the profit motive of Windcliff Plants is undetectable; my father, possessing a Michigan farmer's genotype, would roll in his grave at the notion. At this juncture in my life, it is not in the slightest my concern. On occasion, however, it *would* be nice to at least believe we are breaking even.

Maria Peterson is the woman behind the scenes in our endeavors. Once my assistant propagator at Heronswood, she now organizes my incoherent approach to producing a plant at Windcliff. Twice in the process, she has had the audacity to become pregnant with her husband Jeff and leave me to my own devices as they have produced two gorgeous girls, Ida Lynn and Willa Sue. Both girls suggest that excellent genetics do not in truth vary considerably from one generation to the next.

After my return to Heronswood, Maria and I together, by some bizarre means of understanding without communicating and with considerable help

Seed-grown plants of *Agapanthus* and *Eucomis* that originated in the garden at Windcliff.

from Robert, have arrived at an interesting offering of plants that grow very well at Windcliff. These represent only the plants that I want to grow. Too infrequently do they leave by means of pecuniary transactions.

The nursery has allowed us to explore and investigate new means of propagation, both sexually and asexually. Perhaps, for the sake of marital harmony, I should rework that sentence. Maria and I have sought better pre-germination conditions for seeds, better seed-sowing mixes, better timing for the rooting of cuttings and divisions, and more successful growing-on techniques. This energy of thought and potential for failure would have been unthinkable at Heronswood, as we simply had no time for such frivolous matters. I am not certain that we have made much headway in breaking the code. Seeds germinate or don't, and we don't know why. Cuttings root easily one year and not the next. While plants live sometimes and make us happy, we remain frequently perplexed when they do not.

Flats in the nursery contain cuttings of plants we have decided to produce clonally—that is, to duplicate fully in a genetic sense. I remain as excited as I was as a child when giving a gentle tug to any cutting and discovering it has put down its own root system.

In numerous ways, my small, not-for-profit nursery at Windcliff has become what I had hoped to achieve in my moderately sized, unwieldy nursery at Heronswood. There I had become a manager and office worker in an orbit around the garden that grew more distant as time went on, farther each year from what I loved. The smallness and neatness, the tidiness and purpose of my mindful operation at Windcliff has brought me back to center, while taking me back full circle to the madness of managing two jobs with an occasional third and fourth, all while downing a fifth.

But now, if I might be quite sober for a moment, as I stand again among my seed tables and inspect the pots of germinating seed, I will tell you the truth. I will continue to wonder if what I have done in my life's pursuit, in my undying need to travel and to collect, to propagate and distribute, is right or misguided. What if the seed I returned with, from that quiet jungle or beside the roaring froth of a glacier-fed river, simply wanted to be left where it was ordained to be? But the seed, the plants, are now with me, for good or worse, and any good that might arise from this point on is completely up to me. Whatever bad they might do from this point on is completely because of me. Still I do what I do, I did what I did, because I believe the good holds the upper hand. I believe that gardening is good, and that it all begins with the seed.

Wild Collection

THROUGHOUT THIS BOOK I make frequent and seemingly cavalier references to my collections. Citing those plants in my garden that are directly from my work in the field is second nature to me—it is a language I speak with many of those I associate with. For the uninitiated, it may seem as if I am blithely yet proudly showing off my collection of pre-Columbian art from tombs I have unearthed.

There will always be philosophical disagreements regarding cultivating solely native plants versus those originating outside of our garden's regions. And assuredly, there will be those who read this who are troubled by the possible introduction of invasive plants that will negatively impact the biodiversity of the woodlands and meadows adjacent to their gardens. Their concern is not only warranted but also too infrequently acknowledged by the American gardening and nursery industries. We must accept that we possess not only the opportunity to decipher the natural world in our gardens but also the potential to introduce unwanted species into our native ecosystems.

Generally, when collecting, I gather fifty or fewer seeds per collection, following the rules and regulations attached to my import permits. Careful

ABOVE · Second-generation seeds of the rare *Magnolia sapaensis*, originally collected in Vietnam in 2013 and already blossoming in the garden, are sown at Windcliff.

ABOVE RIGHT · Kevin Carrabine, great friend, assisted me in collecting *Cotoneaster* along the Milke Danda in Nepal in 1995. The resulting plants still politely thrive at Heronswood and Windcliff.

attention is paid to potential bio-invaders if the genus or family has showed those proclivities; those possessing a known potential for bio-invasion are not collected at all. All seed must be fully cleaned before being sent for inspection by the USDA.

The evaluation of a plant's invasive potential is paramount in my process, and it is becoming increasingly important as this journey continues. Yet I believe that we can respectfully enjoy botanical marvels in our gardens while protecting the natural ecosystems that surround us.

Conservation through collection is also of increasing importance in this quickly changing world. Regions I had come to know on intimate terms—by

THE NURSERY

individual plants—have become unrecognizable as economies boom and forests are leveled. Conservation through collection might be nothing more than nonsensical justification, but it does provide a hallmark of the diversity within any ecosystem at any particular point in time. Knowing what we have lost may possibly result in preventing further loss.

Stepping lightly is the best approach, said my late and great friend, Dr. Sarah Reichard, whether in regard to the introduction of new plant species or the vagaries of simple everyday life. A joint responsibility for respecting our world rests with the gardener and plant enthusiast as much as with the nurseryman and plant hunter. Together we can enjoy gems from the natural heritage of our planet while maintaining reverence for that which remains intact outside of our gardens.

A Case Study of *Eucomis* in the Eyes of a Lazy Nurseryman

A TINY CONGREGATION of plants in the asparagus family, some eleven or twelve species all told, members of the genus *Eucomis* are found naturally in the moist meadows, woodlands, and river margins of the lower third of the African continent, geographically centered throughout the Drakensberg Mountains of South Africa and the mountainous nation of Lesotho.

Perhaps one of the most tantalizing scenes I have encountered during innumerable trips looking at plants in the wild was in the Drakensberg Range of South Africa in 2003. On one particular late summer's day, a long hike with dear friends Ketzel Levine and Keith and Ros Wiley led us high into lush meadows chock-full of an enormous assemblage of plants familiar to virtually every gardener. With a playful troupe of baboons spying on us from a distance, we found ourselves within the covers of a sophisticated full-color nursery catalog: *Agapanthus*, *Diascia*, *Dierama*, *Nerine*, *Crocosmia*, *Leonotis*, and *Schizostylis* were among the many species in flower. Yet it was an expansive colony of the curiously beautiful pineapple lily, *Eucomis autumnalis*, presenting thousands of its signature blossoms in hues of bright green suffused with purple, that made the moment so indelible. It was all the invitation I needed to explore in greater detail this remarkable genus of plants.

In varying degrees, purple-foliaged forms of *Eucomis comosa*, with narrow upright foliage and white tubular flowers composed of fused petals surrounded by purple-tinged tepals, have been in cultivation for decades, awaiting the selection of a superior seedling. Selected by Tony Avent, 'Sparkling Burgundy'

Flowering atop a single upright stem per *Eucomis* bulb, elongated heads with clusters of white, green, or purple starlike flowers are capped by a signature coma (tuft) of leaflike bracts. The overall appearance is that of a fanciful pineapple.

inspired renewed interest in the genus and is an honest descriptor of the foliage. It is particularly good in the sultry Southeast, less so in the Pacific Northwest, although its upright, intensely wine-colored blades are sufficiently ornamental to more than compensate for any shortcomings in flower.

Eucomis bicolor, as its name suggests, presents visually stunning pale green petals margined in purple (in some seedlings appearing completely purple) atop fifteen-inch stems, while the somewhat later blossoming *E. autumnalis* offers near-plastic heads of green flowers with a darker green hat capping stems rising to eighteen inches.

In turn, *Eucomis autumnalis* subsp. *clavata* offers genetics of compactness, with prostrate rosettes of broad green foliage and short racemes of flowers. We have used this sensational variety to parent hybrids with *E. vandermerwei*, whose purple-suffused foliage and flowers could use a bit more substance as well as ease of cultivation.

The most ornamental of all of the more diminutive species is *Eucomis humilis*, much too infrequently seen in gardens, with rosettes of extremely broad foliage from which arise one-foot scapes of large white flowers in early September. I am committed to working purple into the foliage of this species as well, extracted from both selected hybrids and other species with naturally occurring pigmentation.

During my first visit to Sissinghurst Castle in the late 1980s, I remember being visually hammered by the architectural presence of *Eucomis pallidiflora* subsp. *pole-evansii* (aka *E. pole-evansii*) with glistening green-and-white flowers capping a thrust of stem to more than four feet. Because it was cultivated at the base of a protected brick wall, I made the assumption that the plant must be tender and deliberately avoided seeking it out for my garden. But now, thirty years later, despite the exertions of a blistery, blustery bluff above the Puget Sound, it performs as captivatingly at Windcliff as it did on that late-summer day in southeastern England when I first made its acquaintance tidied up against a warm wall. The flowering stems of our garden plants, often rising to five feet or more, are harvested before the first frosts of November lay them ruin and are brought indoors for weeks of enjoyment in a very tall vase.

On the bluff at Windcliff grow highly appreciated colonies of a superlative hybrid between *Eucomis pallidiflora* and the previously mentioned *Eucomis comosa* 'Sparkling Burgundy', created by Ed Bowen and commemorating his home state in its nomenclature, 'Rhode Island Red'. It possesses the best traits of both parents—sturdy, erect, plum-colored foliage to three feet and slightly taller scapes with pink flowers capped by a purple coma.

By comingling numerous species, cultivars, and hybrids in close proximity on the bluff, I have essentially put them all in a blender each summer, assisted

Broad, upright, sturdy spears of *Eucomis pallidiflora* foliage are effective as textural accents with *Molinia caerulea*, *Canna indica*, *Crocosmia*, and *Agapanthus*. The eruption of pineapple-like inflorescences from their crowns will ultimately rise to six feet by mid-October.

by a couple of hives of honeybees. The resulting open-pollinated seed is collected and grown on. Our passive selection process has resulted in a plethora of plants deserving further evaluation. Within two years, I am amid hundreds of seedlings and a sparkle of variously hued flowers. *Eucomis* is among the few perennials we replicate clonally by leaf-segment cuttings, taken from selected clones in early August.

Truthfully, most *Eucomis* species are not hardy in the open ground below zone 7, although growing them in leaner, winter-dry sites such as under south-facing eaves in gravelly soil can push their hardiness. However, for gardeners in the north, pineapple lilies—especially the dwarf selections—make exceptionally easy containerized plants. Though they are late to emerge, often not until June, they blossom dependably, are equally handsome in ripened fruit well into autumn, and are easily overwintered if kept dry and protected from extreme temperatures.

Planted as a lark and expected to perish during its first winter, *Eucomis pallidiflora* has become one of the most highly valued components of the late-summer bluff garden, especially effective when backlit in late afternoon by the setting sun. Flowering stems, still intact in early November, are cut and brought indoors for a superlative, long-lasting display.

We are particularly drawn to the dark-hued flower stems of this lot, which we have planted out for more study.

Encouraged by the performance of my initial plantings of *Eucomis pallidiflora*, I increased my holdings by leaf cuttings. This has at last resulted in a healthy colony at the base of our prayer flags, peaking in blossom in early to mid October.

Paradise from Four-Inch Pots

It has been said, and rightly so, that anyone wanting to raise a child successfully should first be required to raise and love a puppy. This should also apply to gardeners. Not the part about a child, as a true gardener's child will always feel neglected and will almost certainly write scathing books about you after you die. But the part about the puppy. All of my dogs have been the kindest and most tolerant of gardening companions, content in exploring the immediacy of our surroundings while I dig holes and weed and prune. None have yet to write a book about my lack of parenting skills.

But the comparison is really meant to say that anyone wanting to garden should first be required to raise a plant from seed. Watch it emerge neck first from a pot of soil like a grazing gazelle and then stand alert as if cognizant of danger. Often enough, its keen perception of vulnerability while in your hands is perfectly sensible. Then carefully place that seedling in your garden and marvel at its journey through space and time toward maturity.

I write this advice to remind us not only of the remarkable process of germination (please, parents, give your children the pips of oranges and lemons to sow upon their windowsills) but also of plants' innate propensity to grow according to their natural inclinations. One seedling dutifully tended soon enough becomes the trying teenager, the young adult with ambitious goals, the responsible contributor to the common good of society, and then, oh too soon, the sage, the wise and wizened, the embarrassingly large.

Patience is the good gardener's best friend, and lack of patience, her downfall. Begin with a five-gallon or twenty-five-gallon plant and you have flushed away the most rewarding moments of gardening. Will you plant your four-inch pot too close to another? Of course you will. But by far the greatest transgression is a misguided belief that your density of planting combined with your innate design abilities are somehow flawed. They are not. Plant as you would raise your child or train your puppy, knowing that all you do in its inception, all you observe and note in its coddling, will pay off in dividends beyond your greatest hopes. Plant small, give wide berth, plant what you love, plant with a passion, and always take great pride in the results.

The
Meadow

We took possession of a stale, parched and pounded, turf-dominated site in 2000. The property had an overwhelming view but was starved of biodiversity. Between the existing mature rhododendrons and bits of established garden, Windcliff's six and a half acres were bereft of life.

This is not meant to sully the memory of two lovely people nor remotely suggest that Peg and Mary disliked biodiversity. I believe that they certainly appreciated and were aware of its concepts more than most in their generation—or even those in my own generation. Times have changed, as they must, and the entirety of our gardens need to adapt in form and function to a world begging for enlightened composers in charge of what is created surrounding our homes, traffic circles, road verges, and office buildings.

In early to mid May, *Camassia leichtlinii* renders the meadow blue while concealing the retreating foliage of earlier performers, including galanthus, primula, lathyrus, muscari, erythronium, and fritillaria. The emerging foliage of *Gunnera tinctoria* provides textural contrast.

Illusions commend themselves to us because they save us pain and allow us to enjoy pleasure instead. We must therefore accept it without complaint when they sometimes collide with a bit of reality against which they are dashed to pieces.

—SIGMUND FREUD

ARMED WITH A FEW DECADES of horticultural experience, I was certain I understood what I was up against in my attempt to create, if not indeed recreate, a socially acceptable substitute for the lawn—my meadow nouveau. After all, I had had the opportunity to study and admire ecologically intact meadows in nature in many different places under significantly different circumstances.

I was off to a remarkably good start, at least in referencing my diminutive personal inventory of good starts, when the miserable dégringolade of my nascent meadow began. I stopped mowing the concoction of grasses, lawn daisies, buttercups, and false dandelions to provide a visual outline of where the meadow would be.

This was to be a meadow of remembrance, of walks through the easy English landscapes—contrived as they were—of Christopher Lloyd and Fergus Garrett at Great Dixter in East Sussex, as well as Keith Wiley's experimental plantings at The Garden House in Devon, owned and managed by the Fortescue Garden Trust. To be fair, though they adopted and perfected the concept, the awakening had begun much earlier throughout Europe with a commitment to landscapes of ecological integrity. The trend has since branched, with Piet Oudolf of the Netherlands leaning toward the mostly aesthetic, and landscape architect Thomas Rainer, to name just one of the front-runners in North America, more eager to simulate or evoke natural communities, with beauty becoming secondary to the intended effect of biological diversity.

*

SO, BACK AT WINDCLIFF . . . lacking Google maps or any discernible written directions, precisely what route would I take? I strongly suggest you do not tailgate, as you will see I am prone to slamming on my brakes and turning without a signal, any conceivable maneuver to avoid pain.

In the Pacific Northwest we are afforded the climatic opportunity to have something in bloom virtually year-round. It is not surprising that the earliest bulbs and herbaceous perennials to blossom—often in early to mid winter—are quite diminutive, as grasslands, their natural haunts, are dormant then and do not obscure the nectar-rich flowers from passing pollinators. *Erythronium revolutum*, *E. oregonum*, *E. multiscapideum*, *Crocus tommasinianus* (and hybrids), *Galanthus* species and selections, dwarf *Narcissus* species and hybrids, *Cyclamen coum*, and even the charming English lawn daisy, *Bellis perennis*, all would blend artfully into the informal yet highly contrived, exuberantly planted, low-cropped "turf" and give a long progression of color twelve months a year.

The Meadow Uncanned

It is an odd thing, the lawn. Is it simply a domestic conflict no one wishes to have, awaiting a truce that everyone longs for?

If we have successfully jettisoned the anachronisms of superfluous fashion and etiquette—at least on the West Coast, where suits, ties, and fascinators are long past—then why do we hold onto such an embarrassingly consumptive landscape practice that offers nothing beyond a realtor's perception of a quick and easy sale? Other than in the case where we create and maintain a horizontal space for us and our children and pets to play, are we not slaves to the process simply because we are expected to be?

Suppose that we all resentfully wage this turf battle, at an immense cost to everything that is truly important for this planet, for a questionable image of idealized suburban life. One must wonder if the reason we do it at all is that our imaginations are taxed and the alternatives too complicated and too risky to consider. In the end, we are all too concerned about what the neighbors will think without contemplating the palpable harm we are doing to ourselves.

Turf might easily be compared to a patient deliberately maintained in a perpetual coma, complete with associated and shuddering health care costs. In a time of soaring fuel prices, profound global climate change, and political instability due, in part, to climate change, consider for a moment the statistics attached to the roots of

our national obsession with a flawless, meaning-less expanse of grass.

Americans quixotically do battle with more than 20,000,000 acres of residential lawns, which are drenched and spattered with 133,000,000 pounds of fossil-fuel-based fertilizer, including 67,000,000 pounds of synthetic pesticides (much of that pre-emptively and needlessly). Lawns are much like an econ-omy; they are either growing or retreating. So we make them grow by bathing them in 30 to 60 percent of this country's urban fresh water (depending on the region).

But, alas, when grass grows, the regimen demands it be cut. By the compressed ignition of 580,000,000 gallons of gas a year, our mowers

wage this battle. Bad-boy SUV statistics pale by comparison. A lawn mower pollutes as much in one hour as does driving an average-sized automobile for 350 miles. And the aftermath winds up in our landfills—some 31,000,000 tons of nitrogen-rich lawn clippings annually, eagerly offloading their leachates into our aquifers.

Mowers are not bad people; some of my best friends are mowers. We simply can no longer afford to pass the ill-advised notion of a perfect lawn on to the next generation.

An aerial shot of Windcliff circa 1961 shows the extent of the comatose turf surrounding the house.

Inspired, we began with a generous patch of our native and profoundly garden-worthy low-elevation fawn lily, *Erythronium revolutum*, already established by Peg and Mary. Over the following fifteen years, we increased the plants to epic proportions by harvesting seed in early June and scattering it throughout the meadow and arboretum at the base of established shrubs and trees. Left undisturbed, these pocket plantings began to blossom and set seed within three years.

Several hundred narcissus were incorporated into the arboretum and surrounding mown turf in 2003. Disappointingly, many of the bulbs were not the diminutive, smart cultivars I had selected but instead 'King Alfred' and other beefy associates that overpowered any evocation of "meadow," similar to too much garlic in a delicate pesto.

I envisioned our native *Camassia quamash* and *C. leichtlinii* offering a stunning river of rich blue atop stems that would sail above grasses emerging from dormancy in late spring. *Dactylorhiza*, the spotted ground orchid, would also

ABOVE · *Camassia leichtlinii* 'Blue Danube' floods the meadow in May.

OPPOSITE TOP · Expanding sweeps of *Erythronium revolutum* formed the beginnings of the meadow at Windcliff.

OPPOSITE · The future meadow in 2003 was planted with several hundred narcissus.

rise through and above the fresh grasses. Clumping asters, in particular the small-flowered species, *Symphyotrichum cordifolium* and *Symphyotrichum ericoides*, would add a distinguished glint of mauve, pastel pink, and white to the meadow in late summer. And autumn bulbs, such as *Crocus speciosus*, *Colchicum speciosum*, *Barnardia japonica*, and *Cyclamen hederifolium*, would come into play in precisely the same location where their spring counterparts had retreated into dormancy.

So there you have it—sensational year-round beauty. A blossoming lawn visited by birds, bees, and butterflies, and even admired by the neighbors, at least when in our presence. A lawn that is long on sound and virtually absent of noise, and one that has drastically reduced the landscape's enabling of the fossil fuel industry.

And absolutely no maintenance.

Wrong. I was never one of the front-runners in this business. I stopped running, short of breath and perilously close to a myocardial infarction, soon after my trials began, all while cursing failure after failure. This could *not* be happening. Not to me, that is. I was, after all, me.

Dactylorhiza spp., the
spotted ground orchid,
rises through and above
the grasses in spring.

My Nisus, My Mettle,
My Muddle

NOW, LOOKING BACK at the images I took of the unshorn turf filled with nonnative weeds in blossom (mostly *Hypochaeris* and *Prunella*) amid a congregation of grass species, also mostly nonnative, and knowing what I know now (Why did no one say?), I should have simply left it alone. My initial response—utter noncompliance with the obligation of mowing—had been the right move. If only I had been brave enough to ignore the calls and comments from neighbors whose homes were on the market.

Now, to even term what I have made, am making, a meadow is an abusage. The sturdier naturalizing bulbs and perennials that were insistent enough to do battle with the existing turf would have waged a successful campaign with our winter-growing grasses had I left them in place. I would already have achieved much of what I sought.

Instead, ever since planting a few dozen misidentified daffodils, I have been recalibrating the process bass-ackward. Admittedly, the meadow movement in the Pacific Northwest was in its infancy at the time I commenced making this "meadow" at Windcliff. And, in all honesty, even if there had already been those who had experimented and failed and from whom I might have learned how to proceed, I would still have imprudently set my own sails, as I wanted the canvas to express my own work. Too bad for me.

Templates to study in the Pacific Northwest *do* exist. A remnant of native prairie known as the Kah Tai Prairie Preserve in Port Townsend sits adjacent to the municipal golf course, ironically the reason the meadow is extant. Another, on Yellow Island in the Orcas archipelago, has a near-identical species mix and shares with the Port Townsend paradigm the fact that it would not have existed, ever, without human intervention. These meadows were maintained as digging fields for quamash, *Camassia quamash* and *C. leitchlinii*, through annual burning by the Salish tribes. Western Washington, unlike Great Dixter and Devon with their shallow chalky soils, will quickly grow an evergreen forest if left, only briefly, to its own devices.

And our climate, gentle and moist in winter, grows grass. *Well.* The mostly naturalized nonnative species will quickly overcome all but the most recalcitrant of annuals and short-lived perennials. My very unenlightened ideal, with willowy drifts of color in perfect sync with the rise of my existing substrate of exotic grass species, was not going to happen.

In the Pacific Northwest, fires deliberately set by native tribes maintained open areas. In the midlands of the continent, massive herds of herbivores kept

Yellow Island, in the Orcas archipelago of the Salish Sea, is known for the springtime floral display of its native prairie remnant.

prairie grasses in check while sufficiently disturbing soils to allow for both reseeding and regeneration. The results were often spectacular displays of spring and summer color. Lacking a moderately sized buffalo herd or neighborhood arsonist, I soon realized that a significant modification of the game plan was in order.

It is much easier to report on my failures than my successes, as the former far outnumber the latter. The abandonment of my civic duties of mowing and blowing was a complete disaster. Our neighbors were just as disgusted with my adamant refusal to perform the weekly task as Robert and I were troubled by the results of our radical departure. Children became afraid to walk down our driveway. Yet I became intrigued enough by nesting sparrows, towhees, and juncos, the proliferation of spiderwebs, and a palpable increase in swallows flying above my untidiness to consider reconsidering my approach.

I had been seeking a ruffled charm—something more handsome than beautiful, like a retired professor's worn tweed jacket, certainly not the dishevelment of an academic gone round the bend. It took only a few visitors who knew what they were doing—okay, they knew what they were doing in their very different climates—to explain where I had gone wrong, long after my train had left the tracks. Thanks, guys.

A young Henri inspects the area of "meadow" that was mulched after initial planting. Inadvertently, rather foolishly, I had just added an acre of cultivated perennial border to my already lengthy list of things to maintain.

Neil Diboll, a long-time horticultural colleague from Wisconsin's Prairie Nursery, took only moments to look at my situation before declaring it an end-stage disaster. "You will never have a meadow," he said, rightfully so. "You like woody plants. The two do not go together." As the old saying goes, you can't have your cake and your ha'penny too.

My mentor from Great Dixter, meadow maestro Fergus Garrett, saw the progress I had made in the spring, before it looked terminally ill. "You have overplanted your camassias," he said. I was outraged. Of course I had overplanted the *Camassia*. "I know that," I replied. I had absolutely no idea how I could have *overplanted* something that was doing such a good job for me, when virtually nothing else I had planted thus far had succeeded in living at all.

The more I attempted to mitigate my mistakes, the more mistakes I made. I planted *Eupatorium purpureum* one year, extracts from the perennial borders at Heronswood. They sung and soared, rising to gargantuan heights while dwarfing the shrubs and trees I had planted throughout the two-acre space. Yes, those would be precisely the shrubs and trees I had been advised to remove entirely. I've had better luck with *Gunnera tinctoria*, hardly an oft-considered meadow plant, which thrives in the winter-wet, summer-dry conditions of the meadow and provides needed ground coverage as well as an admittedly seductive textural additive to the blend of the *Camassia* species at their peak blossom. The gunnera stays put after the bulbs have quit for the summer, providing some, but not yet enough, of the herbage that is so desperately needed.

Lupines, our native lowland *Lupinus polyphyllus*, would be my salvation. They were indeed gorgeous when fully established, mostly on full moon nights when the mildewed foliage glowed in what appeared to be bioluminescence. During the day, they were simply and tragically ugly. And shortly after their period of ugly, they resowed liberally.

Oh lord, the grasses. *Panicum virgatum*. Too tall. *Molinia caerulea*. Too tufted to reliably mow. *Carex pensylvanica*. At its zenith of revolting brownness just as some of the successes were in full blossom; nice complementing tint, I thought to myself. A bit of death thrown into the midst of spring beauty for contrast.

Throughout what now seems to have been an eternity of getting it wrong once and again, I left the ground barren while waiting for the perfect carpet, the silver bullet, to miraculously appear. Once, arriving home through the gate after having been away for two weeks in spring, I glanced across the meadow and was filled with satisfaction. There was a haze of low green taking hold from which my chosen were arising to blossom. Not until later that evening when I went for a closer inspection of my newfound success did I realize the verdant specter was that of thousands upon thousands of germinating big-leaf maples. These all had to be weeded by hand.

A Welcome Entanglement

THERE HAVE BEEN SOME SUCCESSES. Having had my expectations gently lowered by honest friends, I now build upon the realization that a meadow is not what I am making. Not even in the most liberal use of the word.

Running through the difficult thread of wetness that runs the length of the property, *Veratrum californicum* arises from clumps of seductive pleated foliage in early spring and then skyrockets to eight feet in blossom. It loves its feet in the water. I could not grow this successfully at Heronswood, so it is especially satisfying to find it now self-sowing where it wishes to be.

Primula vulgaris subsp. *sibthorpii*, from a collection made in northeast Turkey in 2000, begins the show in December along with *Galanthus elwesii*, *G. plicatus*, and *G. nivalis* 'Pewsey Vale'. The snowdrops continue to bulk in size and throw their white more forcefully each year. Shortly thereafter, the first flowers of *Erythronium revolutum*, pink-flared dancers above purple-mottled

ABOVE RIGHT · *Veratrum californicum* happily grows with its feet in perpetually moist soil.

OPPOSITE TOP · *Veratrum californicum* emerges as *Muscari neglectum* and assorted cultivars of *Anemone nemorosa* are in full blossom.

OPPOSITE · Ground-covering *Ajuga genevensis* and *Anemone nemorosa* are still in blossom as the first flowers appear on *Camassia leitchlinii*.

foliage, begin to appear, by now in the thousands. Charming blue *Scilla siberica*, too, has spread by deliberately scattering its "straw" after flowering. The length of the flowering season of the latter two can be counted by a clock's minute hand during springs when aberrantly warm days appear at the wrong time.

Horticultural associates were skeptical of my integration of *Anemone nemorosa* into the mix, but these plants too have found the space amiable. They blossom in numerous shades, from pure white to deep blue, with a considerable length of effect. The entire show is kaput, leaf and all, by June just as the soils begin to dry.

ABOVE · *Camassia leitchlinii* 'Blue Danube' has its thrilling in-your-face moment in May.

ABOVE RIGHT · A particularly beautiful color form of *Camassia leichtlinii* in the meadow was shared with me by Nutty Lim, a Cornwall gardener of considerable talent with whom I engage in a friendly competition.

OPPOSITE · *Anemone nemorosa* 'Vestal' is one of the latest from the species to blossom and, due to its double-flowered nature, lasts a considerably long time to good effect. The anemones are fully gone in flower and foliage by the latter days of May.

Though I was uncertain when I planted my first tiny consignment of *Camassia* if they would take kindly to the place (we grew them in too much shade at Heronswood to fully understand their charms), taken they have. 'Blue Danube' is the cultivar that gives a thrilling, all-at-once in-your-face moment in May. Unfortunately, the hundreds of bulbs I've planted are clonal in nature and do not set viable seed. I have now sown wild-collected seed among my existing plants to introduce differing colors and blossoming times and encourage seed production. Probably a mistake, but I feel it best to be consistent on my part in committing repeated sins of ignorance. Another caveat: unlike many of the spring ephemerals, camassia has foliage that remains green, yet tattered, for a considerable time, disallowing a cleanup mowing until late July.

The rather vulgar Spanish bluebell, *Hyacinthoides hispanica*, has a foothold at Windcliff from the garden prior to 2000, made worse by the fact that it appears in washed-out shades of pink, white, and mauve, like a wimpy patriotic statement. However, all is forgiven when it comes to the rarely seen long-bracted form, which a keen Irish gardener shared with me years ago. Both the blue and white flowering forms of this unusual aberration are allowed to multiply undeterred and quickly go dormant in summer.

I am still on the hunt for the perfect substrate—the Grand Poobah, the Holy Grail, as good friend and grass guru John Greenlee would refer to it. *Ajuga genevensis* takes considerable foot traffic, can be mown, and tolerates the dryness of our summer months but is not the silver bullet needed as the ground-level substrate. I'm looking for a sedge or low grass that acts as a handsome foil for spring growth, that usurps the light and nutrients and water needed for the germination of unwanted seedlings, and that will take the transition from full sun or partial shade to full shade as the years carry on. I find immense satisfaction in my search, noting species in the wild and in cultivation that may lead me to my personal nirvana.

Still, I must admit that my admiration for the woody plant over the herbaceous has won this round. There are simply too many shrubs and trees from my recent travels that I must grow. As I used deciduous trees and shrubs, much of the spring display will continue for a considerable time going forward; the meadow, however, in its truest sense, never had a chance. An open space of nothingness is simply too tempting, too testing of my resolve, to prevent me from encroaching upon it with yet another plant that refuses to retreat at summer's end.

ABOVE · The even rarer white-flowered Spanish bluebell, possessing accentuated bracts, blossoms in concert with its blue counterpart.

ABOVE LEFT · A rich blue long-bracted form of *Hyacinthoides hispanica* rises above *Ajuga genevensis*.

Carpinus coreana, collected in South Korea in 1993, proved too dense in foliage for the meadow and must be regularly thinned for successful growth of the surrounding meadow.

Viburnum furcatum, collected on Hokkaido in 2001, begins to blossom in late winter, even as early as mid-February in a warm year, just as the leaves begin to unfurl and stirrings at ground level are getting under way. Spectacular autumn foliage offers a repeat performance. The species is undeservedly scarce in American horticulture. Nestled amicably enough in the meadow planting, a pair of the shrubs provides structure and seasonality, yet throws insufficient shade to cause long-term deleterious effects to the surrounding plantings, all while assuaging my inability to exclude woody plants from the palette.

A young *Magnolia obovata*, also collected in northern Japan in 2001, offers powerfully fragrant flowers in May and holds significant meaning for me. Planted at the margin of the meadow, the tree will ultimately become very large and significantly impact light levels. However, it is unlikely I will remove it, requiring instead that the species mix in neighboring plantings change to adapt

Viburnum furcatum offers spectacular autumn foliage and is undeservedly scarce in American horticulture.

ABOVE · The flowers of *Magnolia obovata* are powerfully fragrant in May.

ABOVE RIGHT · *Aesculus wangii* is one of the rarest trees in the garden and sits dead center in the meadow.

to more shade. One of the rarest trees in the garden, *Aesculus wangii*, has been sited dead center in the meadow, disallowing any possibility that the space will develop as intended.

Some of what I've planted will certainly rotate in and out as I assess their garden merits, but already too many rarities and winners exist in the space for me to sincerely believe I am ever retreating. I will attempt to limit density and consider size, but my dreams of a meadow, of my Dixter wanderings on a Sunday morning, cup in hand, have evaporated.

Swallows are still here in ebullient numbers, skimming above this space and browsing on a low-rise flickering feast of insects that had once been extinguished by the mower. There are more spiderwebs and garter snakes, more ground-nesting birds protesting my presence, more Douglas ground squirrels that tease the dogs with a chip and chatter, more honeybees and dumbledores. And the hideous racket is much reduced, the space no longer engulfed in the cacophony and fumes of two-cycle and four-cycle engines, quiet but for a welcome entanglement of living.

Guardians

of

Memory

The entry drive to Windcliff is flanked on both sides by the remembrances of a peripatetic gardener. A trio of narrow *Picea abies* 'Cupressina', propagated from cuttings by the author in 1983, are mementos from Washington Park Arboretum in Seattle.

The enchantment of gardening, of collecting and cultivating and sharing, has as its greatest asset a remembrance of our existence, moment by precise moment. Other than important birthdays, anniversaries, or other auspicious experiences that are part of living, the circular seasons churn too steadily and seamlessly for us to educe without some deliberation when, how, why, and what has been realized throughout our lives. Individual plants have become my bookmarks in the madness of living life to its fullest on a planet that has the audacity to keep turning.

Or perhaps the acuteness of my recollections is simply a personal defect, a pathology of my cerebral cortex where insignificant moments have been encoded and stored by erratically fired neurons, too disposed to resurface when I witness an opening bud, or smell a flower, or hear a leaf rustle in the wind. Am I alone in reliving past days and moments by botanically ricocheting on a stream of consciousness to our gate each morning? And again in reverse that evening without thinking or even necessarily wishing to remember, am I the only one transported to a place or a moment by the mechanics of memory, recalling conversations and ticks of time that have been biologically stored for immediate retrieval by a simple glance at a single plant? If I am alone—though I doubt that I am, knowing too many good gardeners at ripened ages with intact memories—perhaps I should see a therapist. After all, this is coming from someone who can no longer recall the names of good friends when called upon for introductions at social events.

Even between the gates of the two gardens, I consider it my good fortune that the sight of native or invasive plants conjures phantasms of past moments with people I have benefited from knowing. When I can no longer bear to hear a repeat of the latest odious and abusive tweet from our chief executive on NPR and turn the volume to null, an august conversation with Dr. Sarah Reichard, mixed with laughter, often fills the cab of my Toyota truck as I gaze upon embankments of out-of-place brooms and brambles and remember the bridge she so brilliantly crafted between two communities at odds.

But once I am inside the threshold of either garden, the remembrances intensify to a degree that strains belief. With no fear of losing touch with reality, I am afflicted with flashbacks filled with so much detail, so many nooks and crannies still without need of dusting, I could induct an entire legion of insomniacs into a comatose state within minutes were I provided the opportunity to relate to them the minutiae.

One might easily enough believe that the recollections conjured forth by direct encounters with the plants in my garden are mirthful. Happily, most are. It is, however, an inescapable reality that in living there will be loss. A tree here, a shrub there, were planted as or have since become my requiescat to those with whom I can no longer converse.

It is paramount to state before we commence a walk together, so you might fully comprehend the problem I struggle with to the degree that I do, that this is not an ingenuous game of ping pong. One genus can arouse from torpor many characters and places and times independent of one another. There is a profound absence of linearity, you may notice, in a simple stroll down our driveway.

> I am bound—you are bound—to everyone on this planet by a trail of six people.
>
> —JOHN GUARE

THE ENTRY DRIVE AT WINDCLIFF, a personal arboretum of plants and people, holds sharply honed memories of moments gathered over the course of my thirty-five years in the field. More muted but fully discernible sensory encounters are littered throughout Heronswood, where a walk down any trail is impossible without a conversation with J.C. Raulston, the phantom that haunts a thousand gardens across the country, his voice and chuckle still at full volume, embedded with his love for plants and passion for living. The garden of Heronswood is the garden of his generosity. Heronswood became entirely because of J.C. In addition to the portion of his ashes that sits in an urn in our hall, as I remain unwilling to decide his best final placement, his plants and his memory came along with us to Windcliff. I have since seen many of these plants in their rightful place in their native haunts, bringing him with me to them.

An early morning phone call, a friend, had I heard? The crushing airlessness of sadness, remembering the oddly long goodbye embrace at the Raleigh, North Carolina, airport just four weeks earlier.

I came to know *Stachyurus salicifolius* through J.C. in 1989, one of countless species that he introduced me to, broadening my vocal range off the charts. I once visited him at what is now the J.C. Raulston Arboretum and left with a mind-bending number of plants that he insisted I take to trial. While I was seated on the plane at the gate, an announcement was made that the aircraft was overloaded; there would be a delay. My traveling companion on that day,

J.C. Raulston became a personal friend whose friendship equaled in measure the guidance he provided in my professional life.

Eric Nelson, shot me a telling glance that will always bring an inner laugh, memory layered upon memory.

I first traveled with the British team of Jamie Compton, John Coke, Marina Christopher, and John D'Arcy in 1993 in South Korea. Hosted by expat Ferris Miller at Chollipo Arboretum and guided by the gentle-hearted and vastly knowledgeable Kihun Song, we all became fast friends while I absorbed intricacies of the collection process as quickly as possible.

On a particularly grueling hike on Gyebang-san, I think on some level designed to test my fitness before carrying on together as a group, we came upon a recently felled, champion specimen of *Acer manshuricum*. Commercial collectors working the peninsula at that time had taken nothing but the seed from this aristocratic species closely related to the paperbark maple, *Acer griseum*. As I gleaned the remaining seed from the ground and fallen branches, I felt the same overpowering sadness as I might if coming across an elephant killed only for its tusks.

Calycanthus ×raulstonii, a hybrid between *C. floridus* and the then newly discovered *C. chinensis*, hybridized under the direction of J.C., was named in his honor after his untimely death at age fifty-six. It blossoms dependably and comfortingly each year at Heronswood as well as along the drive at Windcliff.

ABOVE · The pendulous late-winter flowering spikes and narrow evergreen foliage of this *Stachyurus salicifolius*, collected in 2011 on Jinfo Shan in Guizhou Province with Johnson and McMahon, makes it a sensational large arching shrub for along the entry drive, conjuring forth the first time I learned of it through J.C. Raulston.

ABOVE RIGHT · The brilliant autumn color of *Acer manshuricum* DJHK 93120, collected in South Korea, brings back memories of a day of birthing friendship in the field.

Today, *Acer manshuricum* rises above the drive, arching over me as I come and go, a specimen raised from seed from a mindlessly vanquished individual twenty-five years ago and transplanted to Windcliff from the collection at Heronswood upon moving to the property.

Though our time together during that trip was brief, the four of us have remained friends. I was traveling on a dime with those of considerable means and heritage; *Comptonia peregrina*, the sweet fern of my youth in Michigan that perfumed the summer night air, was named for Jamie's great-great-great-grandfather, Henry Compton, Bishop of London. When they deposited me at the ferry to Ulleung Island, where I would continue on alone, I believe they had grown quite weary of searching for a pauper's inn before checking in at their five-star lodgings.

I associate *Sorbus ulleungensis* with that first solo adventure on Ulleung Island in the Sea of Japan. When I returned to that island in 1997, with Tony Avent, Darrell Probst, and the Wynn-Joneses, its antiquatedness had diminished. Only four years after my first visit, the isolated villages I had been required to walk to, or negotiate a ride to on a squid fishing vessel, were connected by roads and automobiles.

I met Sue and Bleddyn Wynn-Jones along a dusty road on the western coast of South Korea during the same trip in 1993. I stood in a damp verge collecting seed of *Iris sanguinea* when a car came to a stop alongside me. Windows were lowered and from the bowels of the interior came a query dripping in such heavy Welsh brogue that I momentarily searched for the few phrases retained from a year in Norway two decades prior. What I mustered was *Jeg har glemt skoen min i Norge*—"I forgot my shoe in Norway." Then Sue began to talk. She has interpreted everything Bleddyn has said to me since, except for those times he has resorted to full-on, agitated Welsh at my expense.

Bleddyn, Sue, and I became a collecting unit that lasted years, until our unit became better served through deep friendship. In 1995, with Jennifer Macuiba and Kevin Carrabine, we carried a copy of *Plant Hunting in Nepal* by Roy Lancaster in our backpacks, followed his route, and took turns reading from it on frigid nights in the cook's tent.

Magnolia sapaensis was an unnamed species when Bleddyn and Sue and I collected it on the slopes of Fan Si Pan in Vietnam in 1999 during our first trip to that botanically fantastical region. It was given species rank in 2011. The

OPPOSITE · *Sorbus ulleungensis*, collected on Ulleong Island in 1993, blazes with autumn color and fruit in the arboretum at Windcliff. My time alone on that secluded island remains vivid to this day.

BELOW · *Magnolia sapaensis*, grown from seed collected in Vietnam in 1999, was given species rank in 2011.

flowers open nocturnally, the first night active as male, the second night receiving pollen as female. It is commonly encountered in northern Vietnam but only at elevations of eight thousand feet and above.

In 1999, and on many trips since, we have shared tents in Vietnam, earthquakes in Taiwan, and encounters with Maoist insurgents while again in Nepal. Robert and I marked the millennial celebrations of 2000 with the Wynn-Joneses in their home at their now widely known garden and nursery, Crûg Farm Plants near Caernarfon, Wales. Later that year, we joined forces again for more time together in Japan before venturing on to Yunnan and Sichuan Provinces in China.

ABOVE · *Holboellia yaoshanensis* HWJ 99635 was collected from above Sa Pa, Vietnam, in 1999, during my first trip to Vietnam with the Wynn-Joneses. Seen here in fresh spring growth, it presented flowers for the first time in the spring of 2019.

ABOVE LEFT · The handsome, burnished spring growth of *Trochodendron aralioides* emerges during flowering on a specimen at Windcliff that represents collections made with the Wynn-Joneses in 1999 in Taiwan.

ABOVE RIGHT · Jamaica Kincaid and Sue Wynn-Jones at the beginning of our trek from the Tumlingtar airfield in East Nepal in 2002.

Bleddyn's drive—one might say possession—is something that must be witnessed. His eye in the field is incomparable to that of anyone else I have spent time with, and he has had an enormous influence on my comprehension of the collection process and the plant kingdom, as well as on gardens throughout Europe and North America. The lessons I have garnered from him are engraved in the initials preceding the collection numbers of some of the best plants I have grown: HWJ (Hinkley, Wynn-Jones), HWJCM (Hinkley, Wynn-Jones, Carrabine, Macuiba), HWJK (Hinkley, Wynn-Jones, Kincaid).

From the start, Sue Wynn-Jones has been a sister, friend, confidante, and, when I once drank alcohol, a high-spirited companion of that realm.

My continual references to her husband, Bleddyn, give Sue unjustifiably short shrift, as nothing would have jived without her organizational skills, steadfastness on the trail, and especially her ready smile that brought to us more often than can be recounted an offering of tea, fruit, and rest in whichever country we found ourselves in together.

Bleddyn kindly understood my initial and irrational fear of heights, encouraging me up and over too many fully exposed cliff faces, crags, and overhangs to bother mentioning. Through it, I developed confidence and my own ability in the field. It is a natural course for mentor and student to part, as we did when I began to test my independent mettle. We have remained brothers in memory and spirit.

Tetracentron sinense DJHC 0575 was collected at moderate elevations on Emei Shan in Sichuan Province with Bleddyn Wynn-Jones in 2000. A trio of this collection holds court along the drive, where visitors to Windcliff inquire of its identity during summer, autumn, and winter alike.

The Fourth Dimension

ON ANY WALK ALONG THE DRIVE, a catalog of wrinkles and folds of time unfurls, intact with places and people. The five hundred and fifty feet from our gate to our front door are embedded with memories enough for my lifetime. If I turn around briefly upon entering the gate in mid-October, and with a thousand-yard stare, I can see the conflagrant foliage of *Vitis coignetiae* infiltrating the Douglas-fir with flames of glossed red, yellow, and gamboge.

Five months into an injudicious midlife crisis, on September 11, 2001, I was staying with a friend in SoHo, Manhattan. While doing abdominal crunches, and while a springer spaniel concerned that I was having a grand mal seizure licked my face, I heard American Airlines Flight 11 gut punch the

I have found that there ain't no surer way to find out whether you like people or you hate them than to travel with them.

—MARK TWAIN

Vitis coignetiae, a grape collected on Hokkaido in 2001, blazes in October as it grows up a Douglas-fir just inside the entry gate to Windcliff. David Franklin's jangseung (Korean totem pole) named "Bear Cub Climbing" rises in the fore.

world as it collided with the North Tower. During the next horrifying hour, I witnessed the second plane's impact with the South Tower and the subsequent collapse of both buildings. Briefly, I was pulled into an unnerving panic of screaming people in the streets. In an instant of shocking clarity, my midlife crisis ended.

I reappeared three weeks later, alone, on Hokkaido, the northernmost island of Japan, agitating through mountain trails in search of lucidity and resolve but mostly looking for a distraction that never came. That year my package of collected seed arrived unperturbed at the USDA APHIS facility for inspection at Sea-Tac but subsequently vanished after it was inspected and posted to Heronswood. Six weeks later, as the result of a mammoth investigation by a kind postmistress in Kingston, Washington, the seeds were located in a storage facility in San Francisco.

My *Vitis coignetiae* grew from that lost package of seed, and time, and people's lives. In its finery each autumn, it brings to mind the profundity it embraces—the souls lost, the hearts reunited.

My wander along the drive also affords me the pleasure of looking back into the formulation of my life as a gardener and stirs my imagination as to what gardening might be long after my death. Along the southern edge of a rock retaining wall grows *Veronica umbrosa* 'Georgia Blue', a selection of this species from what was then the U.S.S.R. made by Roy Lancaster in the early 1990s. Now ubiquitous in gardens throughout Europe and North America, some might say pedestrian, it will always have a place in my garden and my heart, presented to me as a gift from Roy when he and his wife, Sue, visited Seattle twenty-five years ago.

I was certainly an annoying, cloying student in the School of Roy. My first interaction with him was through his book, *Plant Hunting in Nepal*, itself a gift from J.C. Raulston. Published in 1981, the account of his first professional plant exploration trip to eastern Nepal intoxicated me, as it also galvanized my life's pursuits.

I am certain that whenever he got a letter from me, or a telephone call, or notice that I was "planning a visit," he and his wife, Sue, were justly mortified. But he—they—remained gracious and welcoming and encouraging, and for that reason I have attempted to pay it forward to those following my own less deeply imprinted footsteps. His contributions are writ large in the United Kingdom, and as he is among the most celebrated of living horticulturists in the world, he needs no nod of approbation from me. Yet, it is proper for me to acknowledge the veneration I hold for him, amply filling at least one full chamber of my heart.

It seems like only yesterday that a motley crew of twelve like-minded plant-driven individuals reconnoitered at the no longer extant Kai Tak International Airport in Hong Kong, watching in disbelief as arriving and departing aircraft seemed to clear surrounding apartment buildings by mere feet.

Tony Avent, a former student and disciple of J.C. Raulston, was among that sleep-deprived dozen; our storyline in life runs parallel to an uncanny degree, each beginning our respective nurseries (his was Plant Delights) in the same year while evolving in our passions at a nearly identical tempo. There too sat dazed Darrell Probst, a great mind of enormous capacity, and Ozzie Johnson, a quiet gentleman from Atlanta whom I had not met before. There were eight more, and to you I offer my apologies as I point to my editor, who insisted you are not significant enough to mention. I protested and still love you.

The China of 1996 was a far cry from the China of the present, though the China of 1996 was not the forbidding, melancholic land of revolutionaries

TOP · *Veronica umbrosa* 'Georgia Blue' in the garden reflects my respect for Roy Lancaster as plantsman, author, lecturer, and plant explorer.

ABOVE · Very few plants in the garden are not infused in some manner with my associations with Roy Lancaster, left, and Bleddyn Wynn-Jones, right. My life in plants would have been overwhelmingly poorer without the inspiration they both have provided.

OPPOSITE · *Vitis coignetiae*, from seed collected on Hokkaido, Japan, in 2001, dependably develops brilliant colors while provoking memories of a fateful day that autumn.

subsisting on a cup of rice per day painted by our homegrown propaganda machine. The collective sense—made evident by Tony's (very large) suitcase dedicated entirely to M&M's, peanut butter, and numerous variations on the theme of chocolate—was that we were off to conquer Everest while warding off the hypnotic threats of totalitarianism.

The Cang Shan, above Dali in Yunnan Province, offered some of the richest collections on the 1996 trip and our subsequent 1998 trip to the same mountain. It was from this range that Ernest Wilson did much of his collecting in the beginning years of the twentieth century. The ultimate for me was scrumming beneath a recently cut specimen of *Magnolia wilsonii* and eventually discovering one viable seed still enclosed in the current year's receptacle, right where Wilson himself may have walked a hundred years before.

At the end of a fascinating, bonding, laughter-filled, at times mentally demanding excursion, I was left with indelible memories of that passage into

ABOVE · *Dipelta yunnanensis* flowers at Windcliff twenty-two years after my first trip to China with a contingent that would become lifelong friends. It was collected under *D.* aff. *yunnanensis* DJHC 104 from Gan He Ba, above Zhongdian, northeastern Yunnan Province.

OPPOSITE, TOP ROW · *Magnolia wilsonii* DJHC 98369 is shown here in bloom and followed by another turn of interest in early autumn. Its seed is distributed annually through the International Magnolia Society.

OPPOSITE, BOTTOM ROW · *Euonymus clivicola* DJHC 98349, shown here in flower and fruit, was collected on Emei Shan in Sichuan in 1998.

China—its people and culture, absurdly opulent history, and overwhelmingly rich floral diversity. Perplexed as to how I would print my list of collections for APHIS inspection before our departure from Kunming, I was kindly handed a thumb drive by the hotel concierge. I had never met a thumb drive before. Still to this day, I am exposed to technological advances in China long before I encounter them at home.

Darrell Probst, Frank Bell, and I continued on to Sichuan that year, saying so long to our fellow travelers in Kunming and flying to Chengdu. This was an illuminative experience on numerous levels. Darrell's nose in those days detected virtually nothing other than *Epimedium* species, and I became the wealthier in knowledge for being near his side on the trail. It was also my first trip to, and the beginning of a love affair with, Emei Shan, one of four mountains in China held sacred in the Buddhist faith and rich beyond comprehension in plants. Two years later, I was drawn back to the same mountain, this time with friends including Ozzie Johnson and novelist Jamaica Kincaid—Jamaica and I shared a room, raised eyebrows, and became co-conspirators of naughtiness, and this gawky massif began to fully reveal its botanical affluence. I returned for my fifth time on the mountain in the spring of 2019.

Life List

MUCH LIKE READING an unknown author for the first time and afterward searching for additional works, so it goes with plants. A species newly encountered—somehow hitherto obscured from view—sets in motion an all-out frontal assault on discovering its natural range, variation within its ranks, and closely related associates. Each stone turned ignites a self-sustaining sequence of acquaintance, intimate knowledge, and ever-expanding instigation.

I received my master's degree in 1983 with a dissertation on the genus Acer, and my life list of maples seen in the wild, those collected by seed, and those sown in the gardens continues to grow to this day. While on Ulleung Island in 1993, I was thrilled to collect seed of *Acer pseudosieboldianum* subsp. *takesimense*, an inimitable experience during which a flock of the beautiful black wood pigeon, which migrates to the island from Japan each spring to nest, surrounded me. It is a tree, and a moment collecting its seed, that I would never be without. So, from myriad possibilities, it was this very collection I chose for Christopher Lloyd to plant with me during his last visit to the states, two years before his death. Somewhat bemused by my request, which he thought maudlin, he quipped half to himself after the deed was done, "And he died three weeks later." I remain grateful that I insisted he do it.

Plant a garden in which strange plants grow and mysteries bloom.

—KEN KESEY

ABOVE · Christopher Lloyd planting *Acer pseudosieboldianum* subsp. *takesimense* during his first and only visit to Windcliff.

ABOVE RIGHT · *Kalopanax pictus* along the drive was planted by Bleddyn and Sue Wynn-Jones in 2013.

Carrying on the tradition of making friends do the work while I glean the profit of memory, Bleddyn and Sue Wynn-Jones planted *Kalopanax pictus* along the drive in 2013 during their visit to Windcliff for Robert's and my wedding. Seed of the tree was collected in 2011 on Jinfo Shan in Guizhou Province, but this time with Ozzie Johnson and Scott McMahan.

As much as I have droned on about my exemplary capacities for remembering plants and moments, I cannot precisely recall how the unit of Hinkley, Johnson, and McMahan cohered. Together we created a merry band of three, with our times together among the happiest of my life. We went numerous times to Japan, Sikkim, Bhutan, Taiwan, and the provinces of Yunnan, Sichuan,

Guizhou, Hubei, Gansu, and Hunan in the People's Republic of China. There is hardly a plant within the Windcliff arboretum that they have not touched within six degrees of separation.

Ozzie Johnson and I, along with his wife, Jitsuko, whose Japanese heritage opened many doors in nurseries and wild spaces of that country, spent many memorable times together in her country as well as our own. Sadly, Jitsuko became ill while we were on a trip together to the nurseries of Tokyo in the spring of 2000. They spent a festive Christmas holiday with us at Heronswood that December, but Jitsuko passed away only weeks later. Ozzie and I returned to Kusatsu, in the Japanese Alps of central Honshu, the following spring to spread her ashes, during which time I found in the wild a golden-foliaged form of *Weigela florida*. It now grows directly inside our gate as *W. florida* 'Jitsuko's Gold'. She was an elegant woman, sharp witted and affable.

Ozzie (affectionately referred to as OJ), Scott (denoted by numerous splenetic expletives, here redacted, meant to lighten a moment or two along the trail), and I had suddenly found us a team, planning the next venture before the present one was over. We did good work, mostly because our eyes worked independently of one another and we each saw things the other two would have missed. Ozzie had been a hydrangea and fern aficionado for decades, while Scott's passion for magnolias, and trees in general, jived well with my remarkable command of everything else we would ever possibly encounter. Ever. It was through the tag team of Bleddyn Wynn-Jones and Ozzie Johnson that I was browbeaten into admiring the genus *Hydrangea* as much as they did. It will take another lifetime to sort out the nomenclature

ABOVE LEFT · Ozzie Johnson (left), a friend since our first meeting in Hong Kong in 1993, and Scott McMahan (center) were with me on a splendid day along the razorback of Fanjing Shan in Guizhou in 2011.

OPPOSITE · *Hydrangea angustipetala*, collected first with Bleddyn in Taiwan in 1999, is one of the earliest to blossom in our garden, greeting visitors along the drive with an arresting sweet fragrance in spring. It has been given the clonal name of 'Golden Crane'.

of the numerous species collected jointly with Ozzie, Scott, and Bleddyn over the past twenty years.

The fellowship of HJM carried forward, including both spring and autumn trips, for fifteen years, concentrating on central and eastern China as well as northern Vietnam. We frequently visited the same precise areas in multiple years, adjusting our arrival dates earlier or later to capture seed we had missed on previous trips. The ploy often paid great dividends.

Each trip was fruitful beyond measure and about so much more than simply acquiring plants. We bonded as family in the field. The vagaries of age, health, and diverging career paths have slowed but not halted our relationship, one that will grow, if only in my reminiscence, as the trees, shrubs, and vines we collected together come to maturity.

A Tangle of Knots

CONTINUING ON DOWN THE DRIVE, looking left through the arboretum toward the meadow, I untangle more convoluted moments that in turn touch more people. I am compelled to tell the tale of *Aesculus wangii*, one of the rarest trees in my collection and one that I hope would be spared should I die tomorrow and the property be bulldozed for development.

In 2006, I was by myself in Vietnam for more than six weeks. My trusted guide, Uoc Le Huu, and I had covered significant territory and I had collected a surfeit of seed, as it was heavily set that year on virtually every species of plant native to the mountains in the north. On my way out of Hanoi, I crossed paths with Bleddyn and Sue along with Peter Wharton and his wife, Sarah, who were just arriving. Peter was a consummate plantsman and curator of the Asian Garden at the University of British Columbia. Over the years, Peter and I had interacted on numerous occasions and developed a close professional relationship.

Still with me? Hang on, as it gets more complicated. "And vastly more interesting," he says.

Three hundred miles to the north, in a locker at my hotel in Sa Pa, I had left Peter and Bleddyn a cache of my surplus collections. In fact, so plentiful and varied was the treasure, perfectly cleaned and dried, they could have simply retrieved it and called it good for the year. (They didn't.) Among the seeds was a single conker of an *Aesculus* I had found, already dehydrated to infertility. I had had little experience with horse chestnuts and no knowledge of those occurring in Vietnam, so I left it for them to examine.

Going forward in time, in the autumn of 2007 I arrived in Taipei from Tasmania to meet Bleddyn for our second tour of the remarkable island of

There is an inward, formless, inarticulate, almost unconscious, prayer . . . whereby the soul is knit fast to the God whom it has tracked, amidst the tangled underwood of human life. . .

—VINCENT MCNABB

Taiwan. The first evening, he excitedly showed me, and shared, his haul of *Aesculus* from Quan Ba, Vietnam, with a grasp of its identity and scarcity. These he had kept moist in sphagnum.

Now, two weeks earlier, Bleddyn and Peter had serendipitously encountered Ozzie Johnson and Scott McMahan in northern Vietnam and shared a few hikes together. This may sound quite odd, but at that time a chance encounter with another plantsman in Sa Pa was as likely as meeting another parent in the stands of a Little League game. This was OJ's and Scott's first taste of the area, and they were appreciative of Bleddyn's support.

Plant collectors are a curious sort. If anyone believes that Ernest Wilson, in 1899, after successfully collecting seed of the near-legendary dove tree, *Davidia involucrata*, would have shared a bit of it with his contemporary and fellow plant explorer George Forrest had they chanced upon one another in Shanghai, they are decidedly mistaken. These are generally the rules of the game. (Personally, I would have given George a bit of my seed, as every picture that I have seen of him has him cozied up to his dog. Or, then again, maybe not.)

Okay, onward.

In summation: Bleddyn shows Scott his *Aesculus* seed but does not offer him one for his bag. Scott is envious. Uoc senses Scott's disappointment but must remain loyal to Bleddyn. On the railroad platform in Lào Cai, with all those concerned boarding the long night train back to Hanoi, Uoc hands Scott a large bag of—*wink*—"potatoes." Scott misses the wink and immediately discards a large quantity of fresh *Aesculus* conkers into the nearest trash bin, perplexedly wondering, "Why in hell would he give me raw potatoes?"

Scott, Ozzie, and I, joined by my good friend Shayne Chandler of Kingston, Washington, returned to the hills of Sa Pa in 2008 and chuckled aloud as we gathered a small collection of unusually large conkers—"potatoes"—of *Aesculus wangii*, one of the rarest horse chestnuts and at risk from cardamom production practices of the area. Shayne has since shared my tent in some of the most remote areas of Asia—far northern Myanmar and extreme northeastern India—and has developed an extraordinary eye for plants. As I write this in late October of 2019, he and I will depart shortly to northern Vietnam. Soon enough, we will be below that venerable specimen of *Aesculus wangii* in search of its enormous conkers before they are consumed by wild pigs.

Today, two specimens of *Aesculus wangii* thrive at Windcliff, along with two at Heronswood, from two different collections in 2008 and 2014, with perpetual hope for the first flower "next spring."

In the spring of 2018, I reconnoitered in northern Vietnam with colleagues, new and old, to explore in greater depth plants on those mountains that I practically knew on a first-name basis, having acquainted myself with

ABOVE · Unusually large conkers of *Aesculus wangii* are held with pride by Shayne Chandler in 2008 at the base of the parent tree in Vietnam.

ABOVE RIGHT · *Aesculus wangii* established successfully in the garden at Windcliff in 2009 and offers handsome and distinguished foliage.

individual specimens over the years. Douglas Justice and Andy Hill, both from the University of British Columbia in Vancouver, as well as Dan Crowley of the United Kingdom, had been previous traveling mates to the same region. Douglas, Dan, and I share a passion for maples, making time spent exploring together an exquisite experience. On this trip we were joined by Quebecois Thomas Robichaud-Courteau, who was examining the use of drones to study the upper reaches of the dense forests of the region. On a memorable day, I watched mesmerized as a small vehicle hovered 150 feet above us amidst the branches of a venerable specimen of *Aesculus wangii*, cut a flowering branch, and returned with it for further study and pressing. In that very instant, I saw extinguished the glorious days of plant exploration while a door opened to youth unbridled by the heralded but burdensome traditions intact for centuries.

Mementos and Fasteners

AS I NEAR THE BEND OF THE DRIVEWAY, a mountain ash from an extraordinary trek in 2002 extends out into the lane as if to say, "Remember me?" My tentmate for three weeks of hiking into the extremely remote northeastern corner of Nepal was Jamaica Kincaid, my previously mentioned roommate during the 1998 trip to Yunnan Province in China. The incessant nighttime laughter from our tent would prove to be as annoying to our compatriots, the Wynn-Joneses along with ten guides and porters, as we had been to the previous contingent in China.

We were venturing up the Arun Valley that slices between Makalu and Kangchenjunga, and had been forewarned by the American consulate in Kathmandu that the Maoist insurgency was active in the region where we would be trekking, though it was unlikely we would be harmed.

On our tenth night on the trail, still at an irritatingly low and beastly hot elevation, we were stopped by an unwelcoming committee headed by a very angry man in a small settlement where we were told we would be spending the night. As we set camp, agitated negotiations began between our guide, Sonam Sherpa—the same we had used in 1995—and the chief angry man. We could not go forward, we were told, or backward, it was implied, unless we paid a fee of one thousand dollars. As group treasurer, I did as demanded—too petulantly, I was told by my trekking companions—and we left the following morning at the break of dawn before breakfast

Sonam, assuming a replay was inevitable, quickly and quietly altered our course before the next village. We crossed the Arun and headed into higher elevations on goat paths, the blind leading the blind. But on this unexpected detour we slipped into an untrammeled bit of "plantsmen's paradise," a phrase coined by none other than Roy Lancaster. Many fine collections were made because of that political unrest, including the *Sorbus foliolosa* that, like bandits, halts me on the drive when in ripened fruit each year. Jamaica's account of our time in the Himalayas together was published in *Among Flowers: A Walk in the Himalaya* (National Geographic, 2005).

The genus *Carpinus*, that of the hornbeam, seems to be a fastener in my life, the proton around which all of my memories adhere by invisible yet obviously strong forces. Ironwood, *Carpinus caroliniana*, was the first tree I

Sorbus foliolosa HWJK 2049 fruits early, dependably, and handsomely each year, taking me back to two extreme days in northeastern Nepal in 2002.

learned in the woodlands of my home alongside my father when I was a lad. At Heronswood, our now-iconic hornbeam hedge remains. It was concocted from *Carpinus betulus* on a February night of frivolity in 1991, when Rosemary Verey, along with a houseful of other celebrated horticulturists, toppled outside with flashlights to pull and stretch branches in an approximation of our ultimate approach. Earlier, there was the admiration of *Carpinus japonica* growing outside my back door while I was living in the Stone Cottage in Washington Park Arboretum with my dog, Emerson. Later, it was encountering seeds of differing species with aforementioned friends in Nepal, Korea, Bhutan, Myanmar, Taiwan, and China.

ABOVE · *Carpinus fangiana*, here shown in blossom, was a youthful grafted plant, biologically mature and emotionally overloaded, when gifted to me by Doug Justice and Andy Hill of the University of British Columbia Botanical Garden.

ABOVE LEFT · Rounding the bend of the drive, now with my cover blown, I am welcomed by Henri with the homecoming bringing of the shoe.

As I round the bend, a final tree catches my eye before the dogs bound from the door to greet me home. *Carpinus fangiana*, the most beautiful and coveted, has flowered. Grown from seed and introduced to the imaginations of western gardeners by none other than Peter Wharton, it sent the likes of us out to collect more from different locales. I have three other clones in the garden, one of which I collected by seed with Scott and Ozzie in Sichuan in 2008 by lifting a rock in a dry riverbed over which a venerable specimen grew. None have yet blossomed, but I can wait. Peter himself returned from a spring expedition to China in 2008 feeling unwell and lived only weeks longer after a diagnosis of cancer. He left behind a living legacy of his own in the Asian Garden at the University British Columbia, itself overflowing with memories, interconnected to all of us ultimately, no degrees of separation.

The trees and shrubs and vines along our drive are memory provokers and reminders of how little I have ever known or ever will and how much more I would like to still. Through their phylogenies and chemistries, I recall the noun, the adjective, the verb, the conversations I had with those with whom I came to know these plants. They continue to make my departure each morning and my arrival home each evening a small thing of majesty.

The road to Windcliff is lined with trees and shrubs and vines that provoke memories and make arriving home a small thing of majesty.

Village Guardians

My times on the Korean Peninsula were seminal in gaining confidence in the field and a greater knowing of myself. The culture is rich and elegant in its cuisine and customs, houses and tidiness, and the people possess a blessed welcoming nature. It was from my experiences there that I gained an appreciation of their tradition of village guardians, jangseung, erected at trailheads and village boundaries to keep at bay the demons of the world.

When Robert and I decided on an installation based on the guardians tradition along the drive, we had only one artist in mind. A nonnative artist responsible for the resurrection of traditional carving in the local Salish tribes (Suquamish, S'Klallam, Makah, and Duwamish), Duane Pasco, had carved the front door for us at Heronswood, depicting heron and frog. We had already commissioned his one-time student, David Franklin, now a celebrated artist in his own right, for traditional panels inside of the house.

David was exultant to briefly break from the purity of locally held traditions and express in his carving a style respectful to the Korean culture but possessing a contemporary slant. I remain gladdened to leave the demons of the world at the gate as I arrive home each evening and shut it behind me. They sometimes attempt to follow but don't stand a chance.

CLOCKWISE FROM ABOVE

A trio of David Franklin's Korean-inspired totems stand guard along the drive.

"Tentacle" is one of nine jangseung crafted for us by artist David Franklin.

"The Watchman" stands guard along the upper drive.

AFTERWORD:
Finale and Finials

Prayer Flags on the southwestern bluff take command of the upper airspace of the garden, alerting us to the movement of air while celebrating those mentors, parents, and siblings who have gone before us.

THERE MUST BE A BOTTOM LINE to our endeavors. *Pollice verso*? Thumbs up? If swallows come to the garden—to nest or to feed—you have received a blessing and a nod. You have created Eden in all its original complexities and subtleties. Not just a thing of fleeting beauty for us, but a cohesion of all that it should embrace—the pollinator, the spider, the serpent, comfort and safety and seclusion for diversity that we do not see nor will ever fully appreciate. I use swallows as my personal indicator for things I will never notice. You may use your own. If we have re-invited to the table that which has been turned away or unconsidered, we have made a garden. In that, if we have indeed done our job as I hope we have, the inspiration and knowledge gained from, as well as the appreciation and love felt for, those who have led me in the process is fully acknowledged. My gratitude is expressed. Perhaps clumsily. Perhaps in too saccharine a manner.

It began as our yearly ritual upon the untimely death of my oldest sibling and only sister, Amy Jan. Now a staff of prayers has been planted on our bluff for each of four parents and each of our many teachers and mentors—many of

The prayer flags are replaced every year on an auspicious day of remembrance. The flags are fully spent after a year and the cotton material burned, as in Buddhist custom, without touching the earth.

whom did not have the chance to grow as old as they should have, to spread their compassion as they would have.

The *Darchog*, or vertical prayer flags, are believed in the Buddhist faith to be activated by the wind. Each gets plenty of play during its year of active duty on our bluff. The supplications are not to our gods for our purposes but are carried on the backs of winds to promote peace, compassion, strength, and wisdom to all sentient creatures in an all-pervading space.

I returned with the first bolt of prayers in my luggage from northern India, specifically the major Buddhist trading center in Kalimpong, West Bengal, in 2005. I have emptied and refilled my larder numerous times since, as it seems the world is in need of absorbing more prayers each year than the previous. We rotate the colors representing the five elements: blue symbolizes sky or space, white the air and wind, green is wood, red flames with fire, yellow takes us to earth.

The poles are traditionally capped with brightly painted finials in styles that depend on their regions of origin. Ours are topped by those traditionally found in Bhutan, bearing a sword indicating wisdom atop the orb of the sun and the moon—the circular nature of life—that rests upon a lotus flower representing eternity.

Each year we watch the cotton gauze slowly lose its substance in the relentless gales of winter, feeling gratified that certainly within a year their meanings have entered countless streams and eddies of air and circled back once or twice to be refreshed.

And when will my own be planted? None of us has a written guarantee for tomorrow neatly folded into our hip pocket. This actuality makes for a steady study of the magic and miracle that surrounds me—in the landscape, the tiniest flower, the fly that annoys, the rabbit that consumes my mahonia overnight.

So for the time being, the winds blow and I watch the flags come alive with their purpose. While I live, I will continue to attempt to make the meadow work as the meadow it will never be and take joy in the successes and bewilder myself with my mistakes throughout this property. I will divide the *Camassia* and *Anemone* and hope that the *Dactylorhiza* will become weeds. I will continue to hope that next spring will bring the first flowers of *Aesculus wangii* and my collections of *Carpinus fangiana*, and that at last I will have the vegetable garden of my dreams.

I will weed the never-ceasing onslaught of *Clematis vitalba*, *Epilobium*, and English ivy. And I will be perplexed by what lives during the next winter storm or summer drought and equally by what perishes. I will again place youthful plants in four-inch pots too closely. The trees that survive will grow taller, and in the process the sun that enticed me to this land from the shadows of Heronswood will be diminished.

Ultimately this garden will belong to another. It will become a pentimento, with another veneer added, as it has been and should be. The fire pit and the grand fir on our bluff will be reabsorbed by the Salish Sea. This line of rubble called the Kitsap Peninsula will last longer, but not forever. Nor will Mount Rainier forever rise to capture the mind-bending colors of our sunrises and sunsets.

But now, while I still live and have the strength to garden on a brilliant day in early June, I will remember again in every pore that time when as a young child I watched the germinating pip of an orange on my windowsill and the first dandelion blossoming in melting snow beneath a crooked box elder that grew in a small village in Michigan called Evart.

A prayer is sent aloft for creatures of all sizes.

Acknowledgments

THE SPECIFICITY OF GRATITUDE IS A RISKY BUSINESS, and there will be those I have forgotten to mention before the orchestra begins to play and forces me from the stage. Forgive me.

I am indebted to the Port Gamble S'Klallam Tribe for acquiring Heronswood and entrusting me with helping to move the garden forward. Fairy-tale endings do sometimes happen, and the story of my first garden offers as close to one as can be found. I thank tribal council chairman Jeromy Sullivan and executive director of the tribe Kelly Sullivan for their welcome and leadership, and especially Joan Garrow, executive director of the Port Gamble S'Klallam Foundation, for her tireless commitment to Heronswood. Returning to my first garden while making my second has brought me immeasurable joy.

Along with numerous other contractors used, we are appreciative of Jim Savage and Colin Nordstrom in the execution of our terrace and water features, along with Alan Hanson, who aided us a thousand times in installation and repair of our irrigation system. Our friend Mark Shorn volunteered his time to aid Robert in construction of our greenhouses.

We are indebted to the artistry of Jeffrey Bale, Mark Bulwinkle, Marcia Donahue, David Franklin, and Dave Kaster shown in their creations found throughout the garden.

How did I deserve the numerous volunteers who generously appeared at Windcliff to give a helping hand before or during benefit events and the massive undertaking of planting the meadow? My thanks to Jesse Ackermann, Cathy Atkins, Dave Demers, Dustin Gimbel, Sarah Gruver, Susan Picquelle, and Gayle Richardson, among others.

Eduardo Montes, who aids me in the garden two days a week, is a gentleman and a quiet, contemplative, and gentle soul who works harder than anyone might ever imagine.

Maria Peterson, with her steadfastness, self-direction, love of plants, curiosity, and extremely hard work, has made making my second nursery a rewarding process.

Duane West, my co-conspirator at Heronswood and great friend for more than forty years, helped to shape my ideas of good gardening and being a decent human being. I will always consider him my brother.

It was pure pleasure working with my editor, Lorraine Anderson, who guided me with gentle questions to make my writing appear as if English were my first language. Thanks, too, to Andrew Beckman and Tom Fischer of Timber Press for instigating the writing of this book.

Fellow gardener and wordsmith Linda Herzog lent her eyes for a perusal of this manuscript.

Lorene Edwards Forkner took on the position of chief organizer and whip. Her ability to help draw this book from me, especially at an extraordinarily busy and convoluted time in her life, will always be deeply appreciated. She helped beyond words to congeal the outline, approach, and text. Thank you.

The photographs of Claire Takacs in this book have brought to these pages the work of a dedicated artist, allowing me the opportunity to see my garden through a set of gifted eyes. I remain in awe of her talent.

And last, most important, none of what I have accomplished in my life would have happened without Robert L. Jones, my lion and love, hose mover, plant puller, reader, truth sayer, and champion.

Photo Credits

ALL PHOTOS ARE BY CLAIRE TAKACS, except for the following:

DANIEL J. HINKLEY, pages 8, 10, 11, 18, 20, 21, 22, 24, 31, 33, 42, 45, 58 (top), 81, 82, 111 (left), 126 (right), 138, 150, 153 (left), 154, 158 (left), 160 (top), 166, 186, 192, 194, 198, 199, 205 (right), 217, 218, 221, 222, 224 (top), 235, 241 (right), 242 (right), 245 (bottom), 247 (bottom right), 249 (left), 250, 255 (left), 259, and 267

Index

DANIEL J. HINKLEY is the creator of the fabled garden at Heronswood and has won a reputation as one of the foremost plant collectors of our time. Among his awards for lifetime achievement are the Arthur Hoyt Scott Medal from the Scott Arboretum, the Liberty Hyde Bailey award from the American Horticultural Society, and the Veitch Memorial Medal from the Royal Horticultural Society. In 2019, the Daniel J. Hinkley Asian Maple Collection was named in his honor by the University of Washington Botanic Gardens. His lectures are legendary, and his current garden at Windcliff, on Washington State's Kitsap Peninsula, is renowned for its audacious design as well as for its deft use of rare, fascinating plants.

CLAIRE TAKACS is an Australian photographer who loves to capture the beauty and essence of gardens and landscapes around the world, particularly while working with light. She sees gardens often as works of art and believes in their ever-increasing importance in our daily lives. Her work is widely published in magazines internationally and she is a regular contributor to *Gardens Illustrated*. She won the Inaugural International Garden Photographer of the Year Award in 2008 and each year continues to be recognized for her work. Her 2017 book Dreamscapes chronicles 70 of her favorite gardens. She divides her time between Australia, Europe, and the United States.

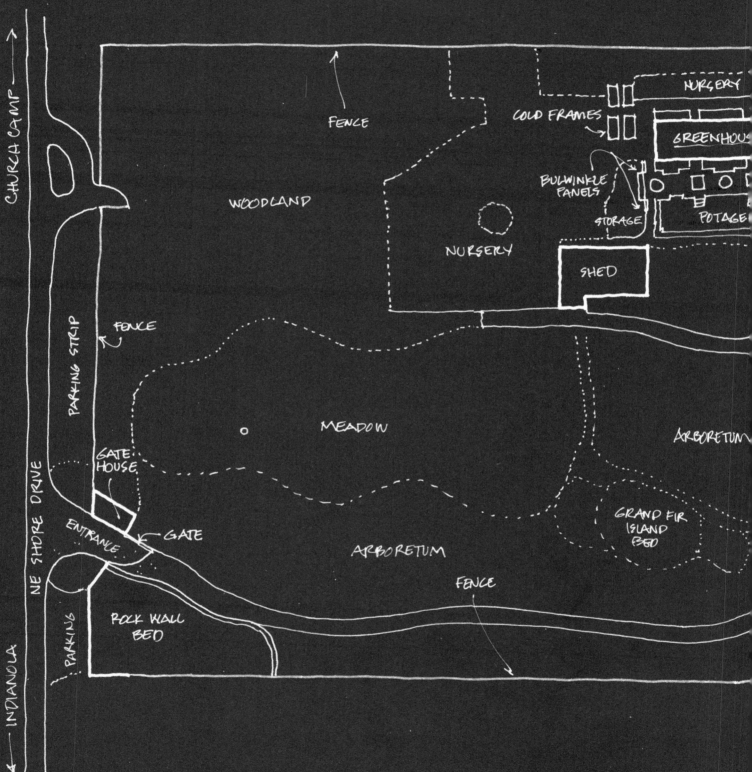